HMH SCIENCE DIMENSIONS™
FORCES, MOTION & FIELDS

Module K

This Write-In Book belongs to

Sarah Quevedo

Teacher/Room

Garvey / 201

Houghton Mifflin Harcourt™

Consulting Authors

Michael A. DiSpezio

Global Educator
North Falmouth,
Massachusetts

Michael DiSpezio has authored many HMH instructional programs for Science and Mathematics. He has also authored numerous trade books and multimedia programs on various topics and hosted dozens of studio and location broadcasts for various organizations in the United States and worldwide. Most recently, he has been working with educators to provide strategies for implementing the Next Generation Science Standards, particularly the Science and Engineering Practices, Crosscutting Concepts, and the use of Evidence Notebooks. To all his projects, he brings his extensive background in science, his expertise in classroom teaching at the elementary, middle, and high school levels, and his deep experience in producing interactive and engaging instructional materials.

Marjorie Frank

Science Writer and Content-Area Reading Specialist
Brooklyn, New York

An educator and linguist by training, a writer and poet by nature, Marjorie Frank has authored and designed a generation of instructional materials in all subject areas, including past HMH Science programs. Her other credits include authoring science issues of an award-winning children's magazine, writing game-based digital assessments, developing blended learning materials for young children, and serving as instructional designer and coauthor of pioneering school-to-work software. In addition, she has served on the adjunct faculty of Hunter, Manhattan, and Brooklyn Colleges, teaching courses in science methods, literacy, and writing. For *HMH Science Dimensions™*, she has guided the development of our K–2 strands and our approach to making connections between NGSS and Common Core ELA/literacy standards.

Acknowledgments

Cover credits: (magnet) ©Houghton Mifflin Harcourt; (maglev train) ©Bernd Mellmann/Alamy.

Section Header Master Art: (waves, computer artwork) ©Alfred Pasieka/Science Source

Michael R. Heithaus, PhD

Dean, College of Arts, Sciences & Education Professor, Department of Biological Sciences
Florida International University
Miami, Florida

Mike Heithaus joined the FIU Biology Department in 2003 and has served as Director of the Marine Sciences Program and Executive Director of the School of Environment, Arts, and Society, which brings together the natural and social sciences and humanities to develop solutions to today's environmental challenges. He now serves as Dean of the College of Arts, Sciences & Education. His research focuses on predator-prey interactions and the ecological importance of large marine species. He has helped to guide the development of Life Science content in *HMH Science Dimensions™*, with a focus on strategies for teaching challenging content as well as the science and engineering practices of analyzing data and using computational thinking.

Cary I. Sneider, PhD

Associate Research Professor
Portland State University
Portland, Oregon

While studying astrophysics at Harvard, Cary Sneider volunteered to teach in an Upward Bound program and discovered his real calling as a science teacher. After teaching middle and high school science in Maine, California, Costa Rica, and Micronesia, he settled for nearly three decades at Lawrence Hall of Science in Berkeley, California, where he developed skills in curriculum development and teacher education. Over his career, Cary directed more than 20 federal, state, and foundation grant projects and was a writing team leader for the Next Generation Science Standards. He has been instrumental in ensuring *HMH Science Dimensions™* meets the high expectations of the NGSS and provides an effective three-dimensional learning experience for all students.

Program Advisors

Paul D. Asimow, PhD
Eleanor and John R. McMillan Professor of Geology and Geochemistry
California Institute of Technology
Pasadena, California

Joanne Bourgeois
Professor Emerita
Earth & Space Sciences
University of Washington
Seattle, WA

Dr. Eileen Cashman
Professor
Humboldt State University
Arcata, California

Elizabeth A. De Stasio, PhD
Raymond J. Herzog Professor of Science
Lawrence University
Appleton, Wisconsin

Perry Donham, PhD
Lecturer
Boston University
Boston, Massachusetts

Shila Garg, PhD
Emerita Professor of Physics
Former Dean of Faculty & Provost
The College of Wooster
Wooster, Ohio

Tatiana A. Krivosheev, PhD
Professor of Physics
Clayton State University
Morrow, Georgia

Mark B. Moldwin, PhD
Professor of Space Sciences and Engineering
University of Michigan
Ann Arbor, Michigan

Ross H. Nehm
Stony Brook University (SUNY)
Stony Brook, NY

Kelly Y. Neiles, PhD
Assistant Professor of Chemistry
St. Mary's College of Maryland
St. Mary's City, Maryland

John Nielsen-Gammon, PhD
Regents Professor
Department of Atmospheric Sciences
Texas A&M University
College Station, Texas

Dr. Sten Odenwald
Astronomer
NASA Goddard Spaceflight Center
Greenbelt, Maryland

Bruce W. Schafer
Executive Director
Oregon Robotics Tournament & Outreach Program
Beaverton, Oregon

Barry A. Van Deman
President and CEO
Museum of Life and Science
Durham, North Carolina

Kim Withers, PhD
Assistant Professor
Texas A&M University-Corpus Christi
Corpus Christi, Texas

Adam D. Woods, PhD
Professor
California State University, Fullerton
Fullerton, California

Classroom Reviewers

Cynthia Book, PhD
John Barrett Middle School
Carmichael, California

Katherine Carter, MEd
Fremont Unified School District
Fremont, California

Theresa Hollenbeck, MEd
Winston Churchill Middle School
Carmichael, California

Kathryn S. King
Science and AVID Teacher
Norwood Jr. High School
Sacramento, California

Donna Lee
Science/STEM Teacher
Junction Ave. K8
Livermore, California

Rebecca S. Lewis
Science Teacher
North Rockford Middle School
Rockford, Michigan

Bryce McCourt
*8th Grade Science Teacher/Middle
School Curriculum Chair*
Cudahy Middle School
Cudahy, Wisconsin

Sarah Mrozinski
Teacher
St. Sebastian School
Milwaukee, Wisconsin

Raymond Pietersen
Science Program Specialist
Elk Grove Unified School District
Elk Grove, California

You are a scientist!
You are naturally curious.

Have you ever wondered . . .

- why is it difficult to catch a fly?
- how a new island can appear in an ocean?
- how to design a great tree house?
- how a spacecraft can send messages across the solar system?

HMH SCIENCE DIMENSIONS™

will *SPARK* your curiosity!

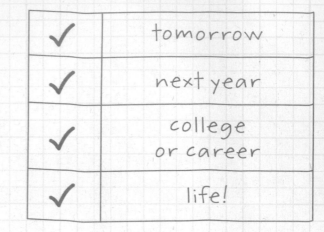

AND prepare you for

✓	tomorrow
✓	next year
✓	college or career
✓	life!

Where do you see yourself in 15 years?

Observe

Collect Data

Be a scientist.
Work like real scientists work.

Analyze

Be an engineer.
Solve problems like engineers do.

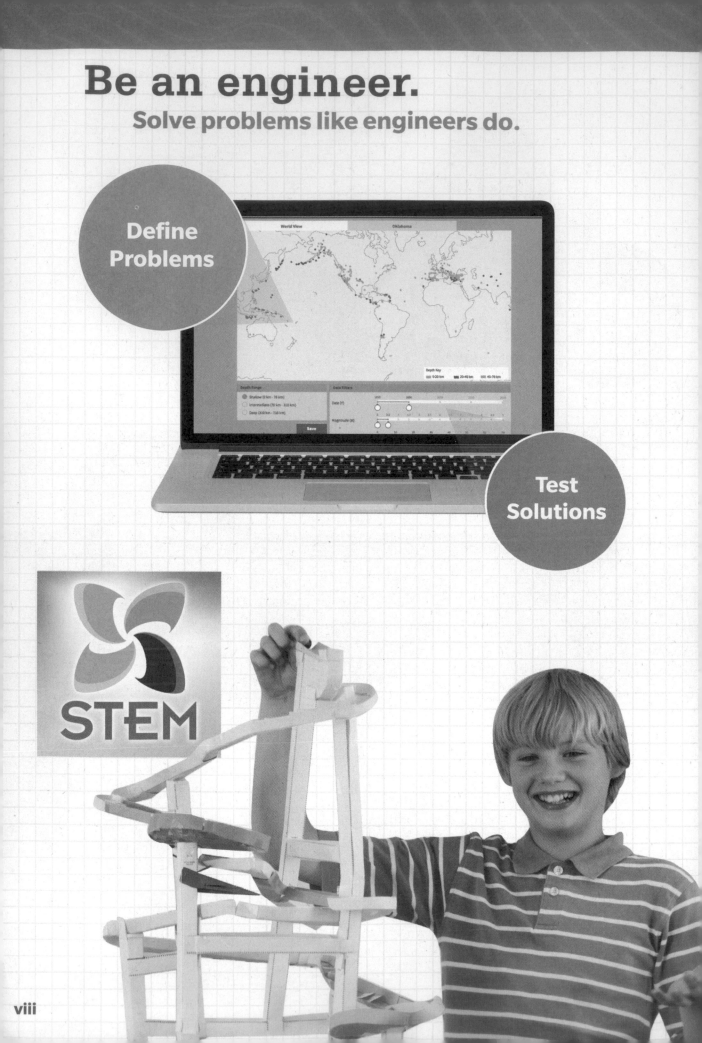

Define Problems

Test Solutions

STEM

Gather Information

Think Critically

Conduct Investigations

Explain your world.
Start by asking questions.

Collaborate

Develop Explanations

Construct Arguments

There's more than one way to the answer. What's YOURS?

YOUR Program

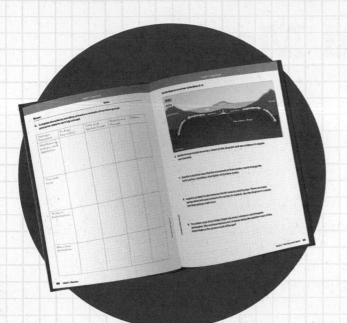

Write-In Book:

- a brand-new and innovative textbook that will guide you through your next generation curriculum, including your hands-on lab program

Interactive Online Student Edition:

- a complete online version of your textbook enriched with videos, interactivities, animations, simulations, and room to enter data, draw, and store your work

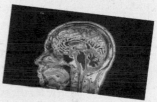

More tools are available online to help you practice and learn science, including:

- **Hands-On Labs**
- **Science and Engineering Practices Handbook**
- **Crosscutting Concepts Handbook**
- **English Language Arts Handbook**
- **Math Handbook**

Contents

UNIT 1 1

Forces and Motion

This swimmer's feet push off against the wall of the pool, and the wall pushes back against the swimmer's feet.

UNIT 2   93

Electric and Magnetic Forces

Iron filings line up along the magnetic field. Scientists use observations like this one to make models of magnetic fields.

Whether you are in the lab or in the field, you are responsible for your own safety and the safety of others. To fulfill these responsibilities and avoid accidents, be aware of the safety of your classmates as well as your own safety at all times. Take your lab work and fieldwork seriously, and behave appropriately. Elements of safety to keep in mind are shown below and on the following pages.

Safety in the Lab

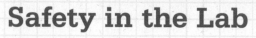

- ☐ Be sure you understand the materials, your procedure, and the safety rules before you start an investigation in the lab.

- ☐ Know where to find and how to use fire extinguishers, eyewash stations, shower stations, and emergency power shutoffs.

- ☐ Use proper safety equipment. Always wear personal protective equipment, such as eye protection and gloves, when setting up labs, during labs, and when cleaning up.

- ☐ Do not begin until your teacher has told you to start. Follow directions.

- ☐ Keep the lab neat and uncluttered. Clean up when you are finished. Report all spills to your teacher immediately. Watch for slip/fall and trip/fall hazards.

- ☐ If you or another student are injured in any way, tell your teacher immediately, even if the injury seems minor.

- ☐ Do not take any food or drink into the lab. Never take any chemicals out of the lab.

Safety in the Field

- ☐ Be sure you understand the goal of your fieldwork and the proper way to carry out the investigation before you begin fieldwork.

- ☐ Use proper safety equipment and personal protective equipment, such as eye protection, that suits the terrain and the weather.

- ☐ Follow directions, including appropriate safety procedures as provided by your teacher.

- ☐ Do not approach or touch wild animals. Do not touch plants unless instructed by your teacher to do so. Leave natural areas as you found them.

- ☐ Stay with your group.

- ☐ Use proper accident procedures, and let your teacher know about a hazard in the environment or an accident immediately, even if the hazard or accident seems minor.

Safety Symbols

To highlight specific types of precautions, the following symbols are used throughout the lab program. Remember that no matter what safety symbols you see within each lab, all safety rules should be followed at all times.

Dress Code

- Wear safety goggles (or safety glasses as appropriate for the activity) at all times in the lab as directed. If chemicals get into your eye, flush your eyes immediately for a minimum of 15 minutes.
- Do not wear contact lenses in the lab.
- Do not look directly at the sun or any intense light source or laser.
- Wear appropriate protective non-latex gloves as directed.
- Wear an apron or lab coat at all times in the lab as directed.
- Tie back long hair, secure loose clothing, and remove loose jewelry. Remove acrylic nails when working with active flames.
- Do not wear open-toed shoes, sandals, or canvas shoes in the lab.

Glassware and Sharp Object Safety

- Do not use chipped or cracked glassware.
- Use heat-resistant glassware for heating or storing hot materials.
- Notify your teacher immediately if a piece of glass breaks.
- Use extreme care when handling any sharp or pointed instruments.
- Do not cut an object while holding the object unsupported in your hands. Place the object on a suitable cutting surface, and always cut in a direction away from your body.

Chemical Safety

- If a chemical gets on your skin, on your clothing, or in your eyes, rinse it immediately for a minimum of 15 minutes (using the shower, faucet, or eyewash station), and alert your teacher.
- Do not clean up spilled chemicals unless your teacher directs you to do so.
- Do not inhale any gas or vapor unless directed to do so by your teacher. If you are instructed to note the odor of a substance, wave the fumes toward your nose with your hand. This is called wafting. Never put your nose close to the source of the odor.
- Handle materials that emit vapors or gases in a well-ventilated area.
- Keep your hands away from your face while you are working on any activity.

Safety Symbols, continued

Electrical Safety

- Do not use equipment with frayed electrical cords or loose plugs.
- Do not use electrical equipment near water or when clothing or hands are wet.
- Hold the plug housing when you plug in or unplug equipment. Do not pull on the cord.
- Use only GFI-protected electrical receptacles.

Heating and Fire Safety

- Be aware of any source of flames, sparks, or heat (such as flames, heating coils, or hot plates) before working with any flammable substances.
- Know the location of the lab's fire extinguisher and fire-safety blankets.
- Know your school's fire-evacuation routes.
- If your clothing catches on fire, walk to the lab shower to put out the fire. Do not run.
- Never leave a hot plate unattended while it is turned on or while it is cooling.
- Use tongs or appropriately insulated holders when handling heated objects.
- Allow all equipment to cool before storing it.

Plant and Animal Safety

- Do not eat any part of a plant.
- Do not pick any wild plant unless your teacher instructs you to do so.
- Handle animals only as your teacher directs.
- Treat animals carefully and respectfully.
- Wash your hands throughly with soap and water after handling any plant or animal.

Cleanup

- Clean all work surfaces and protective equipment as directed by your teacher.
- Dispose of hazardous materials or sharp objects only as directed by your teacher.
- Wash your hands throughly with soap and water before you leave the lab or after any activity.

Student Safety Quiz

Circle the letter of the BEST answer.

1. Before starting an investigation or lab procedure, you should
   A. try an experiment of your own
   B. open all containers and packages
   C. read all directions and make sure you understand them
   D. handle all the equipment to become familiar with it

2. At the end of any activity you should
   A. wash your hands thoroughly with soap and water before leaving the lab
   B. cover your face with your hands
   C. put on your safety goggles
   D. leave hot plates switched on

3. If you get hurt or injured in any way, you should
   A. tell your teacher immediately
   B. find bandages or a first aid kit
   C. go to your principal's office
   D. get help after you finish the lab

4. If your glassware is chipped or broken, you should
   A. use it only for solid materials
   B. give it to your teacher for recycling or disposal
   C. put it back into the storage cabinet
   D. increase the damage so that it is obvious

5. If you have unused chemicals after finishing a procedure, you should
   A. pour them down a sink or drain
   B. mix them all together in a bucket
   C. put them back into their original containers
   D. dispose of them as directed by your teacher

6. If electrical equipment has a frayed cord, you should
   A. unplug the equipment by pulling the cord
   B. let the cord hang over the side of a counter or table
   C. tell your teacher about the problem immediately
   D. wrap tape around the cord to repair it

7. If you need to determine the odor of a chemical or a solution, you should
   A. use your hand to bring fumes from the container to your nose
   B. bring the container under your nose and inhale deeply
   C. tell your teacher immediately
   D. use odor-sensing equipment

8. When working with materials that might fly into the air and hurt someone's eye, you should wear
   A. goggles
   B. an apron
   C. gloves
   D. a hat

9. Before doing experiments involving a heat source, you should know the location of the
   A. door
   B. window
   C. fire extinguisher
   D. overhead lights

10. If you get chemicals in your eye you should
    A. wash your hands immediately
    B. put the lid back on the chemical container
    C. wait to see if your eye becomes irritated
    D. use the eyewash station right away, for a minimum of 15 minutes

Go online to view the Lab Safety Handbook for additional information.

Forces and Motion

This ice skater uses force and decreased friction to glide and spin on smooth ice with his skate blades. The skater digs into the ice with the rough toe picks to propel himself, change directions, and stop.

Ice skating, rowing, martial arts, basketball, and almost all of the other sports you practice or enjoy watching rely on forces that push and pull. Many of the exciting moments in sports that people discuss every day, such as "catching a fly ball" or "nailing a landing," are related to the forces and motion of the athletes. Keep these examples in mind as you answer the Why It Matters questions on the next page. Consider the sports-related phenomena and the questions as you work through the learning experiences in this unit.

Why It Matters

Here are some questions to consider as you work through the unit. Can you answer any of the questions now? Revisit these questions at the end of the unit to apply what you discover.

Questions	Notes
How do you experience friction on a daily basis?	
When do you use pushing and pulling forces in your everyday life?	
What examples of acceleration do you observe on your way to school?	
When have you seen gravity used to make something work?	
What are some examples of tools or objects that apply force?	
What happens when two objects of different sizes collide?	

Unit Starter: Observing Forces in Action

These fairgoers are having fun on a giant slide. Think about the forces acting on the riders as they move down the slide.

1. How could you make the slide more slippery? Choose all that apply.

    A. Slide down on a smoother piece of cloth.

    B. Turn the slide into a water slide.

    C. Go down backwards.

    D. Add sandpaper to the slide.

2. How else could you make people slide down the slide faster?

    A. Decrease the steepness of the slide.

    B. Increase the steepness of the slide.

    C. Increase the number of bumps on the slide.

    D. Decrease the number of lanes on the slide.

 Go online to download the Unit Project Worksheet to help you plan your project.

Unit Project

Collision Course

A force must be applied to an object to make it move. Can you hit a target with a ball without actually touching the ball? Use your knowledge of forces to design a device that will set a ball in motion to collide with a target—but you cannot touch the ball yourself!

Introduction to Forces

A gymnast moves across the beam with grace and strength. During a handstand, she pushes her hands against the beam.

By the end of this lesson . . .

you will be able to model the effects of a force or a combination of forces acting on an object.

CAN YOU EXPLAIN IT?

Which dog will win the tug of war?

These dogs are engaged in a friendly game of tug of war.

1. Look carefully at the two dogs playing tug of war. Each dog is pulling on the rope, but they are pulling in opposite directions. What else do you see? Based on your observations, which dog will win the tug of war? Support your prediction with evidence.

 EVIDENCE NOTEBOOK As you explore the lesson, gather evidence to help explain how forces can help you predict which dog will win the tug of war.

Analyzing How Forces Act on Objects

"The thunderstorm that swept through our town had a lot of force."

"Our team won! It's a force to be reckoned with."

"It took some force, but the janitor finally pried open the stuck locker."

You might have heard the word *force* in everyday conversations, such as in the examples above, but what does it mean in science? In science, a **force** is a push or a pull exerted on an object.

A strong impact can cause a ball to change shape dramatically. The hard golf club was moving at almost 45 m/s when it made contact with the softer driving ball.

2. **Write** Look at the ball in the photo. What has happened to the ball? What caused this change? Use action words to describe what you see.

Suppose you tried to change the shape of the ball in the same way using just your hands. Could you do it? Not likely! It took a very strong force to cause a ball that hard to deform so much. Your choice of action words probably reflected the strength of the forces shown in the photo. Forces of different strengths are all around us. A force can cause a change in an object or in its motion. You can often identify a force acting on an object by observing changes in the object's motion or shape.

Forces

A force is simply a push or a pull. All forces have both strength and direction. Every time you see a change in an object's motion, the change in motion was caused by a force. A force can change the speed or the direction of an object's motion. Scientists measure force using a unit called the **newton** (N).

A backhoe moves a pile of rocks.

▷ *Explore*
ONLINE!

3. How can you tell that forces are being exerted on the rocks in the photo?

Examples of force are all around us. For example, when you pick up a glass of water, you exert a force on it. The force changes the motion of the glass of water from sitting at rest on the table to moving toward your mouth. If you instead pick up a bucket of water, you exert an even greater force. The force you use to move the water glass or the bucket is not the only force acting on the object, though. In most cases, there are several forces acting at once. The combination of different forces acting in different directions determines whether the object's shape or motion will change.

Consider a person sitting still on a chair. Are forces being applied to the chair? Absolutely! The weight of the person is pushing the chair down toward the floor. The chair is also being pulled down by gravity. Both of these downward forces are balanced by an upward force from the floor. The system is stable because the forces acting on the chair are not changing the motion or state of the chair.

The forces acting on this system are balanced.

The forces acting on this system are not balanced.

4. Are forces being applied to the seesaw in both pictures? Explain.

Effects of Forces

When a skater pushes off against a wall, she knows she will experience a change in her motion. Before she puts her hand on the wall, both the skater and the wall are not moving. When she exerts a force on the wall by pushing her hand against it, the wall doesn't move because the force of her push is balanced by other forces on the wall. But the wall also pushes against the skater's hand. The forces on the skater are unbalanced, which causes her to start moving in the direction of the force.

A change in motion is just one of the many effects forces can have on objects. Forces can also cause objects to change their shape. When you walk on grass, you exert downward forces that bend the blades of grass. Think about other ways in which you can change the shape of objects by exerting forces.

The forces shown in the photo are equal and opposite, but they are not balanced because they are acting on different objects.

5. Language SmArts Think about a time when you experienced or used forces. Write a scientific argument describing the situation and the forces that were being applied. Use action words, and be sure to identify balanced and unbalanced forces. Support your explanations with facts.

6. Discuss With a small group, discuss the following scenario: Two birds are flying away from the same tree at the same time. They both fly at 10 km/h for 15 minutes. Why do the birds end up in different places? Summarize your conclusions here.

Velocity and Acceleration

The speeds of the birds in the example were the same, but their velocities were different. *Speed* is the rate at which a distance is traveled. **Velocity** is the speed of an object *in a particular direction*. The sign of a velocity indicates its direction. For a given situation, a velocity in a certain direction is positive, and a velocity in the opposite direction is negative. An object's velocity changes if either its speed or its direction changes. For instance, if a bus speeds up, slows down, or makes a turn, then its velocity has changed. The bus accelerated. **Acceleration** is the rate at which velocity changes over time. Forces can change the motion of objects, so both velocity and acceleration are important quantities in describing forces.

Consider the travelers walking on the moving walkway in the airport. We know the velocity of the walkway relative to the ground and the velocity of the people relative to the walkway. How can we find the velocity of each person relative to the ground? Add the velocities of each person relative to the walkway with the velocity of the walkway relative to the ground. Remember that velocities in opposite directions have opposite signs.

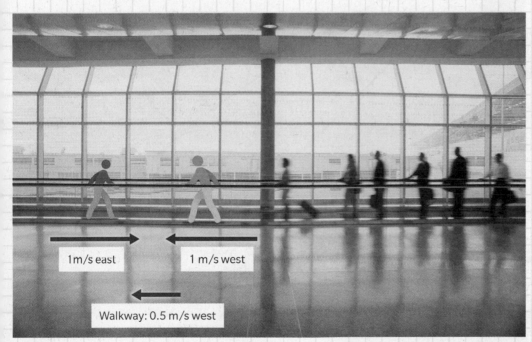

The velocity of each figure relative to the moving walkway is given. The velocity of the walkway relative to the ground is given.

1 m/s east

1 m/s west

Walkway: 0.5 m/s west

7. These stick figures are each in a hurry to catch a flight. They are both walking at a speed of 1 m/s on a walkway that has a velocity of 0.5 m/s to the west. Which stick figure is moving more quickly relative to the ground? Why?

Force Diagrams

What words would you use to describe the forces acting on an object, such as a soccer ball? How would you describe forces of different strengths? Do you think other people will know exactly what you mean? Scientists use *force diagrams* as a way to visually describe the pushes or pulls exerted on an object.

A force diagram is a way to model the forces acting on an object. As you know, force has both strength and direction. In a force diagram, forces are represented by arrows. The point of the arrow shows the direction of the force, and the size of the arrow models its strength. A force diagram can show all the forces acting on an object or system, or it can show only the resultant or unbalanced forces. Study the images below. What forces are being illustrated?

This diagram shows the forces acting on the rocket. The arrow pointing down represents gravity, while the longer upward arrow represents the force pushing the rocket up.

8. **Draw** the correct force arrows to form a force diagram for each of the images shown.

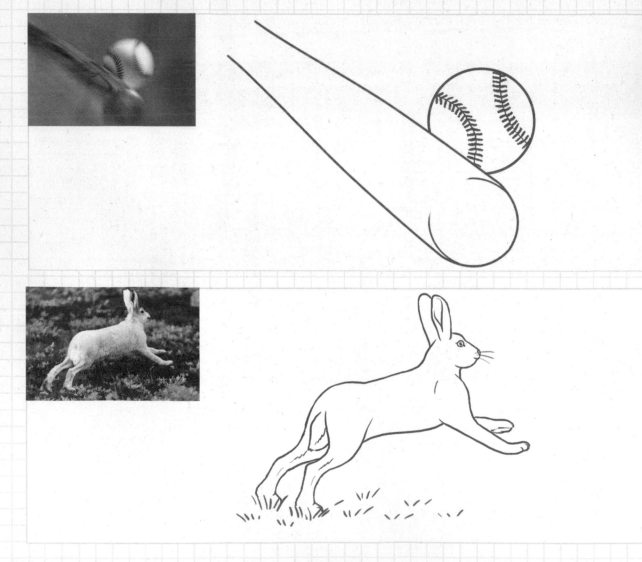

9. Draw a force diagram of the dogs playing tug of war. Which forces will affect the outcome?

Analyze Forces at Work

Imagine a warm and sunny beach. You and your friend decide to enjoy it and go sailboarding. Out on the water, you sail with winds blowing from the east to the west, so you head due west. But then the winds change and blow to the north, so you turn to catch the wind. While you are sailing north, the winds get stronger and push you harder.

Wind blows into the sail of a sailboard, propelling the sailboard and its rider over the water.

10. Apply what you have learned about forces to explain what is happening as you go sailboarding. Describe the forces and how they affect your motion. Do your velocity and acceleration change during the ride? What other effects do forces have?

_____
_____
_____
_____
_____
_____
_____
_____
_____
_____
_____

Investigating Examples of Forces

There are many different examples of forces at work in the real-world. Analyze the forces shown in the following scenarios.

11. **Collaborate** With a partner, discuss each image and then complete the table below. First describe the activity, then identify the effect and the direction of each force, and then diagram the forces. Use a highlighter or some other method to indicate any place where you and your partner do not agree.

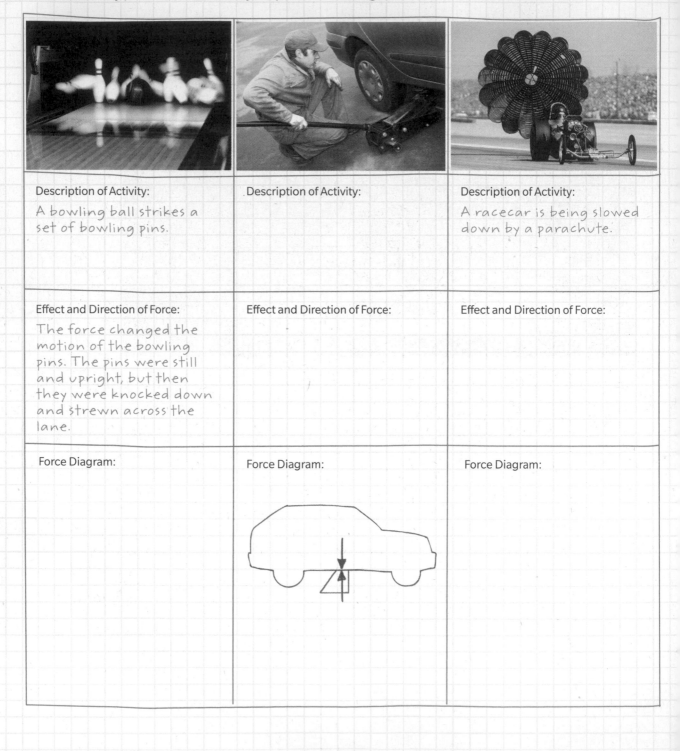

Description of Activity: A bowling ball strikes a set of bowling pins.	**Description of Activity:**	**Description of Activity:** A racecar is being slowed down by a parachute.
Effect and Direction of Force: The force changed the motion of the bowling pins. The pins were still and upright, but then they were knocked down and strewn across the lane.	**Effect and Direction of Force:**	**Effect and Direction of Force:**
Force Diagram:	**Force Diagram:**	**Force Diagram:**

Hands-On Lab
Observe Everyday Forces

Investigate different forces, and make and record observations.

Procedure and Analysis

Visit each of the following activity stations, and carry out the procedures described. Answer the questions, and analyze the forces that are at work.

- Magnetic Forces Station
- Frictional Forces Station

Magnetic force is the force of attraction or repulsion generated by magnetic material.

STEP 1 In the box are several objects, including coins, safety pins, paper clips, and a variety of metal objects. Which objects can be lifted out of the box with a bar magnet? Record your observations.

MATERIALS
- block, wooden
- book
- box
- coins
- eraser, pink rubber
- magnet, bar
- marble
- metal objects
- paper clips
- pencils
- ruler
- safety pins
- toy car

STEP 2 Make a force diagram to model the forces between the magnet and one of the objects that it attracts.

STEP 3 Use evidence from your observations to explain why a recycling center uses a magnet to sort metals.

Frictional force is a force that opposes motion between two objects that are in contact.

STEP 4 Lay the book on the table. You'll use it as a ramp. Place the wooden block on the book at one end, and then slowly raise that end of the book. When the block finally slides down, measure and record the height of the book using the ruler. This measurement is the ramp height for the block. Lay the book flat again. Repeat with other objects, such as a coin, pink rubber eraser, marble, and toy car. Record your observations in the space below.

STEP 5 How do the ramp heights of the different objects compare? How does the ramp height relate to the strength of the frictional force between the book and the object?

STEP 6 Construct an argument to support the statement "You experience frictional forces when you walk down the hall." Describe what would happen if you did not experience frictional forces as you walked.

Contact and Noncontact Forces

Think about the different forces and objects you investigated. Some types of forces only act between objects that are touching. These forces are called *contact forces*. Air resistance is a contact force that acts on an object as it moves through the air. Other forces can act at a distance, such as the force between a bar magnet and a metal object. A force that can act at a distance is called a *noncontact force*.

12. For each of the forces you investigated, use a check mark to indicate whether it is a contact or a noncontact force.

Force Type	Contact	Noncontact
Magnetic		✓
Gravitational		
Air Resistance		
Frictional		

Identify Forces

As you've learned, forces act on all objects whether they're on the ground or in the air.

13. **Draw** Look at the paper airplane in the picture. Predict the path of the paper airplane using force diagrams to explain its motion. Then write one scientific question about forces and paper airplanes that you would like answered.

A paper airplane glides through the air. Its path is determined by the forces acting on it.

Determining the Strength of a Force

You've learned that forces have strength. But how much force is needed for a given task? What determines the strength of the force?

14. **Discuss** Look carefully at the photograph of the woman pushing a lawn mower. With a partner, discuss factors that would affect the strength of force required to push the mower. For example, what effect would the length of the grass have?

Forces Acting on Objects

You have learned that forces can change the shape or the motion of an object, and you have seen examples of forces in action. The change in an object's shape or motion allows you to identify the *net force*, which is the sum of all the forces acting on the object. But sometimes you want to analyze all of the different forces acting on an object.

15. Look at the image of the girl pushing the car. Predict what would happen to the car's motion if someone were helping her. Now look at the image of the woman pushing the box of weights. Predict what would happen to the box's motion if someone were pushing the box in the opposite direction.

Combinations of Forces

Usually more than one force is acting on an object at a time. The combination of all of the forces acting on an object is called the net force. So how do you determine the net force? Add the forces. Forces have both strength and direction. Like velocity, a force acting in a certain direction is positive, and a force acting in the opposite direction is negative. If we decide that forces acting from left to right are positive, then forces that act from right to left are negative. The positive direction is arbitrary for a situation, but once chosen, it cannot change. If both forces are equal in strength but acting in opposite directions, then the net force is zero newtons. If the strengths of the forces are different, the net force will be nonzero and the object will accelerate. The direction of the net force will be the same as the direction of the stronger force acting on the object. The sign of the net force indicates its direction.

Calculate Net Force

Both the smaller person and the bigger person are pushing the box in the same direction: to the right. The forces are both positive, because they are being applied in the positive direction. The net force acting on the box is 50 newtons to the right.

Net force
20 N + 30 N = 50 N
to the right

Here both people are the same size and are pushing the box with the same amount of force and in the same direction: to the right. These forces are positive, since they act in the positive direction. The net force acting on the box is 60 newtons to the right.

Net force
30 N + 30 N = 60 N
to the right

The bigger person is pushing the box to the right, while the smaller person is pushing the box to the left. The forces are applied in opposite directions, so the smaller value is negative, and the larger value is positive. The box moves in the direction of the greater force. The net force acting on the box is 10 newtons to the right.

Net force
30 N + (–20 N) = 10 N
to the right

16. Do the Math In this final scenario, the people are pushing on the box in opposite directions at the same time. Determine the net force acting on the box and in what direction the net force is acting. Show your calculations.

This person is applying 20 newtons of force to the right.

This person is applying 20 newtons of force to the left.

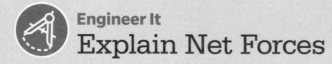

EVIDENCE NOTEBOOK

17. Think about the two dogs playing tug of war. What data do you need to calculate the net force on the rope? Record your evidence.

Engineer It

Explain Net Forces

Have you seen long trains snake through the countryside? Sometimes a train will have two or more locomotives, or engines, pulling it. And, occasionally, a train will have one or more locomotives at the very end.

18. Why would a train need more than one locomotive? Apply what you've learned about forces and net forces to explain what problems might be solved by adding locomotives to a train.

The four locomotives at the front of this train pull the long chain of cars along the tracks.

_____

_____

_____

_____

_____

_____

_____

_____

_____

_____

_____

Continue Your Exploration

Name: Date:

Check out the path below or go online to choose one of the other paths shown.

Roller Coaster Restraints

- **Hands-On Labs** ✋
- **TV Science Advisors**
- **Propose Your Own Path**

Go online to choose one of these other paths.

When you sit in a roller coaster train that is not moving, the force of gravity holds you in your seat. The seat pushes up on you to balance the force of gravity. Think about what happens when the roller coaster train is moving. You accelerate in many different directions, and the force of gravity may not hold you in your seat. Roller coaster designers have designed different types of restraints to keep you safely in your seat as you accelerate during a ride.

Think of a roller coaster train accelerating down a steep hill. Gravity pulls both you and the train downhill at the same rate. The track keeps the train on a certain path, but what keeps you with the train? Restraints may apply forces to keep you safely in your seat as the train moves.

Compare the different types of restraints. Think about the forces that each type of restraint can apply to your body. Some restraints allow you to slide around and even lift off the seat a little. Others hold you firmly against the seat. Think about the hills, loops, and turns roller coasters can have, and when each type of restraint would be appropriate.

A T-bar rotates toward a rider and locks in place. Here a T-bar restraint combines with an over-the-shoulder restraint.

A lap bar restraint lowers and goes across the lap of a seated rider. It prevents a rider from standing up during the ride.

An over-the-shoulder restraint rotates down to fit over the shoulders and sometimes across the chest and waist.

A locking lap bar is similar to a standard lap bar, but more securely locks into place to prevent a rider from falling out.

Continue Your Exploration

1. **Draw** a force diagram of the forces acting on a person while sitting in a roller coaster car as it accelerates up a hill. You may choose the type of restraint.

2. Describe the forces acting on the passenger in your drawing. Explain how these forces affect the motion of the passenger.

3. List the following roller coaster restraints in order from the least restrictive (allows a passenger to move in their seat) to the most restrictive (passengers can move very little): over-the-shoulder, T-bar, lap bar, and locking lap bar.

4. **Collaborate** Research and make a recommendation about what types of restraints an engineer should choose when designing a roller coaster. Present your argument about when each type of restraint would be appropriate and what tradeoffs engineers might need to make when choosing restraints for a roller coaster.

Can You Explain It?

Name: _____   **Date:** _____

Which dog will win the tug of war?

EVIDENCE NOTEBOOK

Refer to the notes in your Evidence Notebook to help you determine which dog will win the tug of war.

1. State your claim. Make sure your claim fully explains how you can predict the outcome of the tug of war.

2. Summarize the evidence you have gathered to support your claim, and explain your reasoning.

Checkpoints

Answer the following questions to check your understanding of the lesson.

Use the photo to answer Questions 3 and 4.

3. Which statements are true about the house of cards on the table? Choose all that apply.

    A. The force of gravity is acting on the cards and the table.

    B. The forces acting on the house of cards and the table are balanced.

    C. The forces acting on the house of cards and the table are unbalanced.

    D. The house of cards is not stable because too many unbalanced forces are acting on it.

    E. The house of cards is stable because balanced forces are acting on it and the forces are not changing.

    F. The house of cards is stable because there are no forces acting on any of the cards.

4. Suppose you pulled a card from the bottom layer. The house of cards would collapse, but why? Choose terms to make the statement true.

    The elastic forces/gravitational forces would cause the cards to be more flexible/to be pulled down toward the table.

Use the photo to answer Questions 5 and 6.

5. The woman is using colorful letters to hold the drawing to the refrigerator. What type of force is pulling the letters toward the refrigerator?

    A. gravitational force

    B. frictional force

    C. air resistance force

    D. magnetic force

6. The force acting between the refrigerator and magnets is a contact / a noncontact force. The forces acting on the sheet of paper are balanced/unbalanced because there is no change in the force / motion of the paper. The net force on the sheet of paper is zero / can't be calculated.

Interactive Review

Complete this section to review the main concepts of the lesson.

A force is a push or a pull and can change the shape or motion of an object. Forces have strength and direction and are expressed in newtons. Balanced forces produce no change in motion. Unbalanced forces produce a change in motion.

A. What do you need to know in order to analyze the forces at work in a situation?

People use a variety of forces in everyday activities. Some forces are contact forces, and others are noncontact forces.

B. How does a contact force differ from a noncontact force? Give an everyday example of each.

Objects usually have more than one force acting on them. The combination of forces is called the net force. Net force is determined by combining forces.

C. What model can you use to represent the forces acting on an object? How can it help you determine the net force on the object? Explain.

Gravity and Friction

Part of the thrill of ski jumping and other extreme sports comes from the weightless feeling as you fall through the air.

By the end of this lesson . . .

you will be able to use evidence to support an argument that interactions involving gravity or friction depend on the properties of objects.

CAN YOU EXPLAIN IT?

Why did the two objects fall together?

See an apple and a feather fall from the same height at the same time. Notice that both objects fall equal distances during each time increment.

1. Do the apple and feather in the image fall as you would expect them to fall? How is the motion different or the same as your expectations?

EVIDENCE NOTEBOOK As you explore the lesson, gather evidence to help explain how forces affect the motion of falling objects.

Exploring Gravity

When you throw a ball into the air, knock a spoon off a table, or drop a pencil, you know what's going to happen. In fact, you have probably been aware for a long time that, unless acted on by another force, objects always fall down. This happens because of gravity.

Do you think this dog has ever studied gravity? He sure seems to know that the ball is going to fall—and where it is going to land!

2. **Act** Work with a group to create a one-act play about gravity. Perform the play for your class. Summarize your play in the space below.

Gravity

For many years, scientists observed the motion of falling objects and the motions of planets. Although they couldn't see gravity, they could see its effects. These observations led scientists to develop models of gravity. **Gravity** is a force of attraction between objects due to their masses. Because gravity exists between objects even when they are not touching, it is called a noncontact force. Gravity is always an attractive force because it always pulls objects toward each other.

A Robot on the Moon	A Robot on Earth
The mass of this robot on the moon is 50 kg, and its weight is about 81 N.	The mass of the same robot on Earth is 50 kg, and its weight is about 490 N.

3. Look at the images of the robot on the moon and on Earth. What do you notice about the robot's mass and weight? Explain your observations.

Weight

Mass is the amount of matter in an object. *Weight* is a measure of the pull of gravity on that mass. Weight is a force. Think of it this way: An object is made up of a certain amount of matter, so its mass is constant. The object has a certain weight due to the force of gravity. If the force of gravity decreases, the weight of the object decreases. If the force of gravity increases, the weight of the object increases.

Mass and weight are measured using different units. A common unit for mass in the metric system is the gram (g) or the kilogram (kg). Scientists measure forces with newtons, a unit named after Isaac Newton. An apple with a mass of about 102 g weighs one newton (1 N) on Earth. The same apple would weigh 0.16 N on the moon.

4. **Do the Math** A scientific instrument has a mass of 54 kg, and its weight on Earth is about 529 N. Jupiter's gravity is about 2.3 times stronger than Earth's gravity. Use this information to calculate the mass and weight of the instrument if it were on the surface of Jupiter.

Gravity near Earth

It is important to know that the gravitational force Earth exerts on you is equal to the gravitational force you exert on Earth. But because your mass is so much smaller, the effect of that gravitational force is much greater on you.

The pull of objects toward Earth is not the only gravitational force on Earth. Every object exerts a gravitational force on every other object. Why do you not normally notice the gravitational pull of other objects? Most objects on Earth have too little mass to exert enough force for us to notice effects. However, the moon and Earth are both large objects with a lot of mass, so the gravitational force between them is large. The tides occur because of gravity and the moon. The force of gravity between Earth and the moon is what holds the moon in orbit around Earth. An *orbit* is a curved path that objects take around a star, planet, or moon. Notice that the surface of Earth is not a perfect sphere. What happens to the force of gravity on an object in a canyon or on top of a mountain?

The surface gravity of the moon is one-sixth of Earth's.

5. Objects near Earth's surface are attracted toward Earth's center / surface. Because of this, if you dig a hole in Earth's surface and drop an object into the hole, the object will continue to fall until it reaches the original surface level / bottom of the hole.

6. **Collaborate** Working with a partner, imagine that you are able to dig a tunnel through the center of Earth to the opposite surface. Describe how gravity would affect you if you jumped into the tunnel. What would happen as you pass the center of Earth?

Hands-On Lab
Investigate Falling Objects: Mass

Predict how changing the mass of an object affects how it falls. Test your predictions and record your observations.

Procedure and Analysis

STEP 1 Fill a plastic bottle about one-quarter of its volume with sand or marbles. Make sure to close the lid to contain the sand or marbles.

STEP 2 Drop the bottle from a height of one meter onto the pillow. Record the time it takes for the bottle to reach the ground. Repeat this action three more times.

STEP 3 Compare the times for each of the attempts in Step 2. Did the bottle take the same amount of time to fall from the same height every attempt? Explain.

STEP 4 Predict what will happen if you fill the bottle one-half its volume with sand or marbles and drop it from the same height as in Step 2.

STEP 5 Fill the plastic bottle half-way. Drop the bottle onto the pillow from the same height as in Step 2. Record the time it takes for the bottle to reach the ground. Repeat this action three more times.

STEP 6 Did your observations support your predictions? If not, what was different?

STEP 7 Based on your observations, what can you conclude about the relationship between an object's mass and the rate at which it falls?

EVIDENCE NOTEBOOK

7. How do your observations in this activity help you interpret the image at the beginning of this lesson of the apple and feather falling? Record your evidence.

Determine the Force of Gravity

When we think about gravity, we usually think about the force that makes objects fall and keeps us from floating off into space. While those effects of gravity are important in everyday life, Isaac Newton described gravity as a force that every mass exerts on every other mass. This model also allowed him to mathematically describe the force two objects exert on one another. The strength of the force between two objects depends on the masses of the objects and on the distance between them.

Effect of Mass on Gravity

Imagine a universe that contains only two objects. Newton showed that the gravitational force between them could be calculated using their masses and the distance between them. If both objects have the same mass, it makes sense that the force each exerts on the other is the same strength. If we increase the mass of both objects while keeping the distance the same, the gravitational force increases. The force of gravity on both objects is equal in strength. If we change the mass of only one of the objects, will both experience the same gravitational force? Yes, the force depends on both masses, and both objects always exert the same amount of force on each other. If we increase the mass of one or both objects, the force between them is stronger. If we decrease the mass of one or both objects, the force is weaker.

Effect of Distance on Gravity

For large objects such as stars and planets, the distance between two objects is measured from the center of one to the center of the other. Imagine that we could easily change the distance between two massive objects while keeping their masses the same. If two objects are moved farther apart, the force they exert on each other decreases. If two objects are moved closer together, the force increases. That is why rockets must travel many kilometers above Earth's surface to break free of Earth's gravity. Even though objects such as Earth and the sun are very far apart, because they are so massive, the gravitational attraction between the two affects their motions. For less massive objects, the gravitational attraction may be very weak, even when the objects are very near. You will feel the gravitational attraction toward Earth more than the gravitational attraction to a person standing next to you.

Diagram of Gravitational Force

8. Draw the force arrows to model each scenario correctly. The first scenario has been done for you.

Analyze Gravitational Force

The graphic shows the force of Earth's gravity on a 50 kg object at different distances from Earth. Analyze the information in the image to answer the following questions.

6,400	12,800	19,200	25,600	32,000	38,400	Distance in kilometers from Earth's center
486	122	54	30	19	14	Gravitational force on a 50 kg object at each location rounded to the nearest newton

9. In the image, the mass of the object *remains constant/* *changes constantly.* As the distance from Earth's center increases, the gravitational force on the object *increases/decreases.*

10. You and your friend are having a discussion about weight. He claims that he weighs less on the 100th floor of a building than he does on the ground floor. Is he correct? Support your answer with evidence.

_____

_____

_____

_____

_____

_____

11. If a 50 kg object is at a location 25,600 km from Earth's center, what is the gravitational force exerted by the object on Earth? In what direction does that force act? Support your answer with evidence.

_____

_____

_____

_____

_____

_____

_____

_____

_____

Exploring Friction

These students are demonstrating the floating rice flask trick. One student is able to lift the flask filled with rice by inserting a chopstick into it. When the other student tries, the chopstick slides out and leaves the flask on the table. See whether you can figure out the forces involved in this mysterious phenomenon.

▷ *Explore ONLINE!*

Friction

The key to this trick is friction. **Friction** is a contact force that resists motion between two objects. The flask that cannot be picked up is loosely filled with rice. The flask that is picked up is tightly packed with rice. The tightly packed rice creates more friction when the chopstick is inserted. This friction between the rice and chopstick allows the flask to be lifted. Try it yourself!

If you have ever tried to push a heavy box across a rough floor, you have experienced friction. Friction is the resistance you feel when you try to push the box. If the box were empty, there would be less friction, and you could more easily push the box. If the floor were smooth, there would also be less friction, and you could more easily push the box.

12. Two similar-size friends encounter a long hallway with a smooth tiled floor. One girl is barefoot and the other is wearing socks on her feet. Apply what you already know about friction to predict which girl would slide farther down the hallway.

Is It Smooth or Rough?

The surface of any object—including paper—is uneven. Look at the magnification of each object and think about how each surface would feel against your finger.

13. **Draw** Examine the model showing the interaction between the surface of a finger and the surface of the wood. Friction is created when the hills and valleys of one surface stick to the ridges and valleys of another surface. Choose one of the other surfaces above, and draw a model of the interaction between it and a finger.

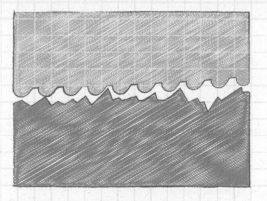

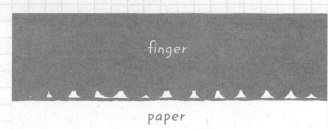

finger

paper

The Effect of Surface Variation on Friction

The friction between two objects depends on several factors. One of the factors is how smooth or rough the surfaces are. A smooth surface creates less friction than a rough surface. Why do rough surfaces have more friction than smooth surfaces? The microscopic hills and valleys of the rough surface are more likely to catch on opposing hills and valleys. This is what increases friction. The smooth surface has lower hills and shallower valleys, so when an object slides across it, there is less for the object to catch on. With less opposition, the object slides easily across the surface.

Hands-On Lab
Investigate Friction

Plan an investigation to support the claim that the types of surfaces affect the amount of friction between two objects.

MATERIALS
- book, lightweight
- paper clips, large
- sandpaper
- string (1 m)
- washers, metal
- waxed paper

Procedure and Analysis

STEP 1 What information do you need to support the claim that the types of surfaces in contact affect the amount of friction between two objects?

STEP 2 Describe how you will investigate this claim. Include your experimental setup, independent and dependent variables, and what data you will collect. Have your teacher approve your plan.

STEP 3 Carry out your investigation. Record your data on a separate sheet of paper.

STEP 4 Explain how your data support the claim.

Friction Affects Motion

Friction opposes motion. Your investigation should show that friction changes between different surfaces. Friction between two surfaces also changes if those surfaces are pressed together more firmly. You may also notice that friction between two surfaces that are not moving is greater than friction between the same two surfaces that are moving. For this reason, the amount of force needed to start an object sliding will keep it sliding.

Depending on the situation you may want to increase or decrease the friction between two surfaces to control the movement between the surfaces. For example, you need friction to keep you stable when you walk, so more friction is desired. The hinges of a door, however, should move freely, so less friction is preferred.

Reducing Friction

Parts that squeak or that don't move freely are showing signs of too much friction. For example, if your bike is difficult to pedal, too much friction between the chain and the gears might be the cause. One way you can reduce the friction is by adding a lubricant, such as oil or grease, to one or both surfaces. The lubricant makes the surfaces smoother so that the parts slide against each other more easily. Now your bike should be easier to pedal!

You also can reduce friction by replacing sliding friction with rolling friction. If you place that heavy box you want to move on a cart with wheels, the box is easier to move. Inline skates move quickly and smoothly across a surface because ball bearings—smooth metal balls between the wheel and the fixed axle of the skate—reduce friction.

Oil is applied to a bike chain to reduce friction between the chain and gears.

Increasing Friction

If there is too little friction, something may move too easily. Picture a car spinning its wheels because there is too little friction between the tire and the road. Rock climbers use special shoes to increase the friction between the shoe and the rock. This increased friction allows climbers to stand on fairly steep rocky surfaces.

Another way to increase friction is to increase the weight of an object. A heavier object exerts a greater force and therefore has more friction. Some people use this fact to prevent their cars from slipping on ice by adding heavy items to the trunk of the car. The increased weight results in greater friction, so the car will not slide as easily.

Climbers wear special shoes to increase friction between the shoe and the rock.

14. For each scenario described below, choose whether friction is increased or decreased.

   A. Ugh! This pan is really dirty. I'm going to have to press down really hard with the scrubber. increased friction/ decreased friction

   B. Oh no! My bedroom door is squeaking. I'm going to use some spray lubricant on the hinges. increased friction/ decreased friction

   C. This cabinet is really heavy and I can't move it. I'll put it on a cart. increased friction/ decreased friction

   D. These shoes are really slippery on this floor. I'll put on shoes with rubber soles. increased friction/ decreased friction

Evaluate Friction

15. **Collaborate** With a partner, discuss how friction affects moving parts on a bicycle. What parts are designed to increase friction? What parts reduce friction? Include suggestions for reducing or increasing friction to properly maintain a bicycle.

_____

_____

_____

_____

Analyzing Forces Acting on Falling Objects

You know that objects fall because gravity pulls objects toward Earth. But do all objects fall to Earth exactly the same way? What are the factors that determine how forces act on falling objects? To investigate this, drop two sheets of paper—one crumpled in a tight ball and the other kept flat. The flat paper falls more slowly than the crumpled paper because of air resistance. Air resistance is the force that opposes the motion of objects through air. So, regardless of an object's mass, the more air resistance there is, the more slowly the object will fall.

16. This skydiver jumps out of an airplane high in the sky. What do you think will happen after the skydiver jumps out of the plane? What will happen after the skydiver opens the parachute?

Hands-On Lab
Investigate Falling Objects: Air Resistance

Design a parachute that will slow the fall of an object.

Procedure

STEP 1 Drop a clothespin or toy figure, and observe how it falls. Examine the materials available and design a parachute to slow the fall of your clothespin or action figure toy. Describe or sketch your design.

STEP 2 Build your parachute.

STEP 3 Test your parachute by dropping the clothespin or toy figure with the parachute and measuring how long it takes to hit the ground. Perform several trials from the same height to make sure your measurements are accurate. Record your results.

Analysis

STEP 4 Compare your design and fall time with those of other groups. Which design fell the slowest? Which factors affected the parachute's ability to slow the fall of the clothespin or action figure toy?

Air Resistance and Falling Objects

Air resistance is friction between a moving object and the air around the object. One way to think about air resistance is to imagine yourself walking through a crowded room. You bump into people, and every collision slows you down. These people and collisions are similar to how air molecules interact with an object to create air resistance. To reduce the frequency of collisions, you might try to make yourself smaller or walk more slowly. Now imagine walking in an empty room. You can walk with your arms outspread without colliding with anything. The amount of air resistance acting on an object depends on the size, shape, and speed of the object and the density of air. The *density* of air is the number of air molecules in a given volume.

17. To slow down the fall of an object, you want to *increase / decrease* the air resistance. To speed up the fall of an object, you want to *increase / decrease* the air resistance. Removing air to create a vacuum, like in space, *increases / decreases* the amount of air resistance acting on a moving object.

EVIDENCE NOTEBOOK

18. Compare the falling objects that you observed and the objects shown in the photo at the beginning of this lesson. How might your observations be used to explain how forces affect falling objects? Record your evidence.

Engineer It

Improve a Parachute

You know objects fall because the force of gravity attracts all matter on Earth toward the center of Earth. Other forces, such as air resistance, can be used to slow the fall of an object.

19. An engineer is developing a new parachute. She conducts a test of a prototype. During the product testing, the object attached to the parachute falls too quickly. How might she redesign the parachute so that the object falls more slowly? Select the correct statements.

   A. Make the parachute less massive, because heavier objects fall faster than lighter objects.

   B. Make the parachute wider to increase air resistance.

   C. No redesign will help. The force on the object due to gravity does not change, so the object will always fall at the same rate.

   D. Increase the surface area of the parachute. Increasing the surface area will increase the air resistance and slow the object's fall.

These skydivers are jumping out of a plane one after another. Notice how the parachutes affect how the skydivers fall.

Continue Your Exploration

Name: _____ Date: _____

Check out the path below or go online to choose one of the other paths shown.

> **Gravity and Space-Time**

> • **Snowboarding and Forces**
> • **Propose Your Own Path**

> *Go online to choose one of these other paths.*

After Isaac Newton published his work on gravity in 1687, there were still a lot of unanswered questions: What causes gravity? Why does gravity always pull objects together when other forces can also push objects apart? Gravity is one of the biggest mysteries in science. In 1915, Albert Einstein published a theory that described gravity in a new way. Einstein explained that space and time are woven together like fabric and that massive objects cause this space-time to dimple or dent. Einstein's theory helped to explain Newton's observations. It also explained some things better than Newton's laws, such as the amount that light bends when it travels past massive objects like the sun. Scientists today are still finding evidence for Einstein's ideas about gravity, such as the recent discovery of gravitational waves. Newton's ideas are still useful for explaining most cases of motion. Like Newton before him, Einstein opened the way to new discoveries in science.

Sir Isaac Newton worked as a servant to pay for college.

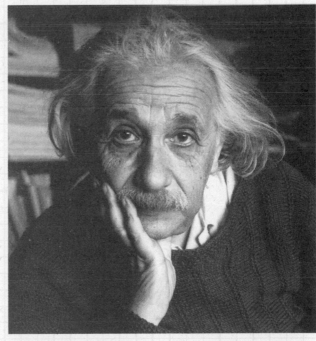

Albert Einstein has a crater on the moon named after him.

Continue Your Exploration

An artist's impression of gravitational waves generated by a binary neutron star system.

1. Picture setting a bowling ball on a trampoline. Describe or sketch what might happen.

2. Next picture holding a second bowling ball a short distance above the first and dropping it onto the top of the first bowling ball. Describe or sketch what you might observe.

3. In the scenario above, the trampoline models space-time. The bowling balls model the collision of two black holes. The vibrations represent the gravitational waves. Identify one limitation of this model.

4. **Collaborate** Together with a partner, research the National Science Foundation's Laser Interferometer Gravitational-Wave Observatory (LIGO). Create a visual presentation that includes a timeline of the program as well as the location and history of each ground-based observatory. Remember to include any plans for future observatories and next steps in the ongoing research.

Can You Explain It?

Name: _____ **Date:** _____

Why did the two objects fall together?

 EVIDENCE NOTEBOOK
Refer to the notes in your Evidence Notebook to help you construct an explanation that describes why the apple and feather fall at the same rate.

1. State your claim. Make sure your claim fully explains why the two objects fall together.

2. Summarize the evidence you have gathered to support your claim and explain your reasoning.

Checkpoints

Answer the following questions to check your understanding of the lesson.

Use the photo to answer Questions 3 and 4.

3. If all three balls have the same mass and size, which statements are true?

    A. Gravity exerts almost the same force on all three balls.

    B. Each ball is equally attracted by gravity to the other balls and to Earth.

    C. Gravity is acting on the two balls in the air but not the ball in the juggler's hand.

    D. All the balls experience similar amounts of air resistance as they move.

4. The juggler replaces the balls with scarves. How would the motion of the scarves be different from the motion of the balls? Explain.

    A. The scarves would fall slower because they are lighter than the balls.

    B. The scarves would fall slower because they have more air resistance than the balls.

    C. The scarves will fall in the same time as the balls because gravity attracts all objects the same.

Use the diagrams to answer Questions 5 and 6.

5. The diagrams show two planets of different masses with identical orbiting satellites. Select all the conditions that would increase the gravitational force between each pair.

    A. Move the satellites closer to the planet.

    B. Move the satellites farther from the planet.

    C. Add mass to the satellites.

    D. Remove mass from the satellites.

6. The density of the planets and satellites shown are the same. The gravitational force between the red planet and its satellite is _more / less_ than the gravitational force between the blue planet and its satellite. This is because the combined mass of the red planet and its satellite is _greater / less_ than the combined mass of the blue planet and its satellite, and the distances between each planet and its satellite are _different / equal._

Interactive Review

Complete this section to review the main concepts of the lesson.

Gravity is a noncontact force that depends on the masses of objects and the distance between them.

A. Describe two ways you can increase the gravitational force between two objects.

Friction is a contact force that opposes motion.

B. Describe a situation where more friction is desirable and a situation where less friction is desirable.

Air resistance is a type of friction that occurs between air and moving objects.

C. Describe the forces that act on a skydiver before and after the parachute is opened.

Newton's Laws of Motion

This longboarder may not realize it, but he is using several laws of motion to get to his destination.

By the end of this lesson . . .

you will be able to model and describe how unbalanced forces cause changes in motion.

Go online to view the digital version of the Hands-On Lab for this lesson and to download additional lab resources.

CAN YOU EXPLAIN IT?

Why does the golf tee fall into the bottle when the hoop is pulled?

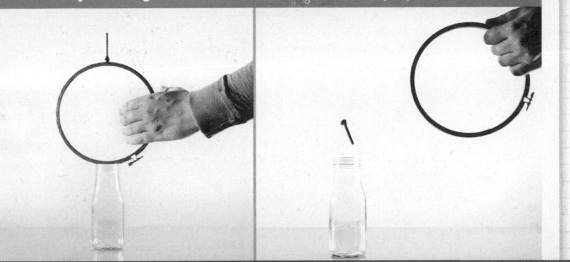

Observe carefully to see how the person can get the golf tee to drop straight into the bottle. Consider what forces act on the golf tee during this event.

▷ *Explore ONLINE!*

1. What forces are acting on the golf tee when it is at rest on the hoop? What forces are acting on the golf tee when it is falling in the bottle?

 EVIDENCE NOTEBOOK As you explore the lesson, gather evidence to help explain the motion of the golf tee.

Describing Motion

Diving into a pool, pedaling a bike, jumping over a puddle, sinking into a comfy chair, biting into a crisp apple—these are all types of motion. **Motion** is a change in an object's position over time. Position describes an object's location. Suppose you were diving into that pool. One moment you are standing tall on the edge of the diving board, and the next moment you are in the air above the water. Finally, you enter the water. During the dive, you were in motion because your position changed over time.

Explore
ONLINE!

A flock of thousands of starlings fly in formation.

2. The starlings flying in formation *are / are not* in motion. The birds' positions are changing over time. The flock's position can be described as being *above / below* the clouds and *above / below* the ground.

3. **Discuss** With a partner, debate whether the couple in the photograph is in motion. Support your claim with evidence. Record the main points of your discussion.

This couple rides a train to get to their destination.

Motion and Reference Points

How can you tell if something you see is moving? You are actually comparing the object's position to that of another object that appears to stay in place. The object that appears to stay in place is called a **reference point**. You can measure the object's motion as its change in position relative to the reference point. You can choose any point you like, as long as you specify what it is. Often it makes sense to choose a set of objects that are all stationary with respect to each other. This set of objects is known as a *reference frame*. In the train example, you could say that the man and woman are in motion because they are moving relative to the scenery outside the train. However, if you used the train car as your reference frame, you could say that they are not moving.

4. You are sitting in a crowded movie theater waiting for friends. The following are ways that you could describe your location within the theater using reference points. Which descriptions may be unreliable because of the reference point?

    A. I am sitting near a theater worker, fifth seat from the side.

    B. I am in the fifth row from the back, tenth seat from the right side.

    C. I am in the sixth row from the front, tenth seat from the right side.

    D. I am in the sixth row, east of the man in a red shirt.

The scout uses radar to measure how fast a ball is pitched.

5. The radar device detects the motion of the ball and calculates its speed relative to
   the pitcher / the batter / home plate / the radar device.

Speed, Distance, and Time

If an object's position changes, you know that motion took place but not how quickly the object changed position. The **speed** of an object is a measure of the distance an object moves in a given amount of time. The unit of speed is distance per time, for example, meters per second or miles per hour. The choice of what units to use when measuring motion is arbitrary but must be specified so the data can be shared with others. The radar device measures the speed of an object over a very short period of time. The actual speed of an object may vary widely or stay relatively constant. We may calculate the average speed of an object over a longer period of time, depending on the equipment available and desired information.

Average Speed

As described previously, knowing that the position of an object has changed tells you that the object moved, but it does not tell you how quickly. Look at the two images of the cars on a track at two different times. You can see that between the first and second image, the red car's position has changed, but this is not enough information to know the speed of the car. Speed involves two quantities: distance traveled and time traveled. So in order to calculate the speed of the red car, we need to know how much time passed between the first image and the second image. We also need to know the distance traveled by the red car during that time. If we know the red car traveled 16 feet during the two seconds between the images, we can calculate the speed of the red car as eight feet per second. But did the red car travel at exactly eight feet per second the entire time? Probably not. This speed is the average speed of the red car during those two seconds. The actual speed of the car during this time may have varied.

Distance vs. Time

The speed of an object can be determined from a graph of distance traveled over time. The blue line in the graph shows the total distance traveled by a car during a four-hour period. The red line shows the distance traveled by a train moving at a constant speed during the same four-hour period.

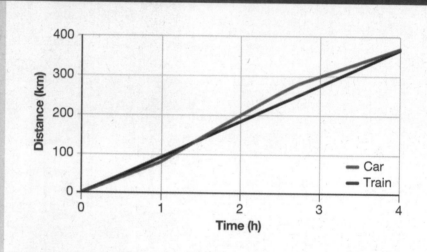

6. Do the Math Use the graph to determine the average speed of the car for the first hour of the trip and for the entire four-hour time period. The total distance traveled for each time period can be read from the blue line on the graph. Estimate the distance traveled to the nearest 10 kilometers.

$$\text{average speed} = \frac{\text{distance traveled}}{\text{travel time}}$$

$$\text{average speed during first hour} = \frac{80 \text{ km}}{1 \text{ h}} = \boxed{80} \text{ km/h}$$

$$\text{average speed for 4 hours} = \frac{\boxed{60} \text{ km}}{\boxed{4} \text{ h}} = \boxed{90} \text{ km/h}$$

Velocity

Sometimes it is necessary to know both the speed of an object and which way it is going. The **velocity** of an object is a quantity that describes the speed of the object and its direction of travel. You can think of velocity as the rate of change of an object's position in a reference frame. An object's velocity is constant only if its speed *and* direction do not change. Therefore, constant velocity is always motion along a straight line. If either an object's speed *or* direction changes, its velocity changes. To indicate the direction of velocity, we use positive and negative numbers. If an object moves in the positive direction, we use a positive number to represent the velocity. If an object moves in the opposite direction, the velocity will be negative. Any direction can be positive or negative, but the choice must be consistent. For example, if a ball thrown upwards has a positive velocity when it travels upwards, it must have a negative velocity when it falls.

7. A bus travels north along a straight stretch of road. Its velocity is a constant 15 m/s. Another bus travels south on the same road at the same speed. What is the velocity of the second bus?

Do the Math

Calculate Resultant Velocity

Suppose you are riding on a train. The train is moving in relation to the ground. If you stand up and walk down the aisle while the train is moving, then you are moving relative to the train and to the ground. To find your velocity relative to the ground, add your velocity relative to the train with the train's velocity relative to the ground. Remember if the velocities are in opposite directions, one will be positive and the other negative.

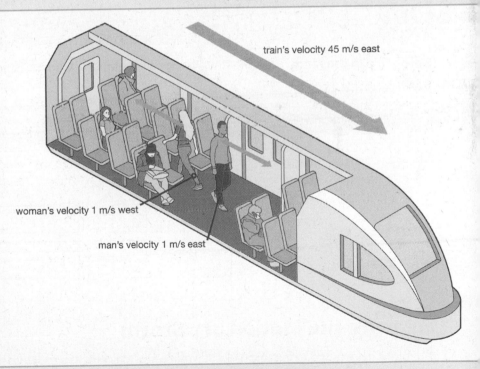

The diagram shows a train car moving at a velocity of 45 m/s to the east. Two passengers are walking on the train. The passengers' velocities relative to the train are shown.

8. Look at the train in the diagram. If the train is moving in the positive direction, calculate the velocities of the man and woman walking in the train relative to the ground.

Acceleration

The rate at which velocity changes is called **acceleration**. Velocity is the rate of change of position; its units are distance per time. If the velocity is measured in meters per second, the acceleration might be measured in meters per second per second, or m/s^2. An object accelerates if its speed, direction, or both change. Like velocity, the direction of acceleration is indicated by using positive and negative numbers. If an object has a positive velocity and its speed increases, it has a positive acceleration. If an object is moving in the positive direction and its speed decreases, it has a negative acceleration. Average acceleration may be calculated in a way similar to average velocity.

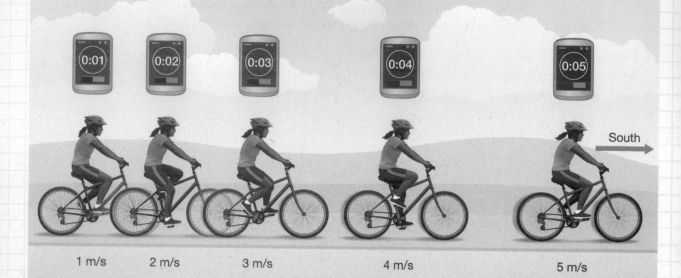

9. **Do the Math** Calculate the average acceleration of the cyclist in the image by using this equation:

$$\text{average acceleration} = \frac{\text{final velocity} - \text{starting velocity}}{\text{time it takes to change velocity}}$$

Use the velocity at 1 second as the starting velocity and the velocity at 5 seconds as the final velocity. South is the positive direction.

average acceleration = $\dfrac{\boxed{}}{\boxed{}}$ = $\dfrac{\boxed{}}{\boxed{}}$ = $\boxed{}$ m/s² south

Measure the Motion of a Storm

You might have heard a meteorologist say that a storm is heading east into your area at 40 km/h. What do you know about the motion of the storm?

10. The speed / velocity of the storm was given as 40 km/h east. This is the speed / velocity because it includes the direction in which the storm is moving in addition to how quickly it is moving. The meteorologist's statement does / does not include whether the storm is accelerating.

Analyzing Newton's First Law of Motion

Imagine that you are playing baseball. The pitch comes in, and—crack—you hit the ball! But instead of the ball flying off the bat, the ball just drops to the ground. Would that really happen? No! The baseball will move away when you hit it with a bat. You know from experiences like this that the force exerted on an object is related to the motion of the object in some way. In 1686, Sir Isaac Newton explained the relationship between force and motion with a set of three laws of motion.

Newton's First Law of Motion

Newton's first law of motion states that, unless acted on by an unbalanced force, an object at rest stays at rest and an object in motion stays in motion at a constant velocity. In other words, if the forces on an object are balanced, the object will not accelerate. Like velocity and acceleration, forces have direction. A force in one direction will have an opposite sign from a force acting in the opposite direction. To find the net force on an object, add the forces. If the forces on an object are balanced, the net force on the object is 0 newtons (N). If the forces on an object are not balanced, the object will accelerate.

11. A force acting on an object in the upward direction is 3 N. The force that would balance this force could be written as ___*newtons*___. We know these forces will balance because 3 N + (__0 N__) = __0 N__. The balancing force acts in the __same__ direction.

The bowling ball quickly moves toward the pins.

12. Look at the photo of the bowling ball and pins. What do you think will happen next?

Objects at Rest

An object whose position is not changing relative to a reference point is said to be at rest. The golf ball balanced on the tee is an example of an object at rest. The upward force from the tee on the golf ball balances the downward force of gravity on the ball. When the ball is at rest on the tee, there are no unbalanced forces acting on the golf ball. Newton's first law says the golf ball will stay at rest until an unbalanced force acts on the ball. When the moving golf club strikes the ball, it applies an unbalanced force to the golf ball. The ball then moves in the same direction as the unbalanced force.

An Object at Rest

The golf ball begins at rest on the tee. When the golf club strikes the ball with an unbalanced force, the ball begins moving in the direction of the force.

Objects in Motion

Newton's first law also says that objects in motion stay in motion with a constant velocity unless they are acted on by an unbalanced force. Recall that if an object moves at a constant velocity, both its speed and direction do not change. Imagine that you are driving a bumper car at an amusement park. Your ride is pleasant—and your velocity is constant—as long as you are driving in an open space. But the name of the game is bumper cars! Eventually, another car hits you, exerting an unbalanced force on your car. As a result, your bumper car stops moving. Note that the *car* stops moving, but not you! You continue to move forward in your seat until the unbalanced force from your seat belt stops you.

An Object in Motion

Bumper cars demonstrate how an unbalanced force can change the motion of a moving object.

Friction and Newton's First Law

Imagine a baseball player sliding into second base. The player must run quickly before sliding and she can only slide for a short distance before stopping. Newton's first law says that an unbalanced force must act on the player to make her stop. What is the unbalanced force that causes the player to stop sliding? Friction. Friction is a force that occurs when surfaces are in contact. The force of friction always opposes motion. To balance the force of friction, it is often necessary for a force to be applied to an object to keep the object moving at a constant velocity.

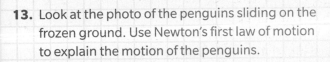
Explore ONLINE!

13. Look at the photo of the penguins sliding on the frozen ground. Use Newton's first law of motion to explain the motion of the penguins.

Emperor penguins slide on the frozen ground in Antarctica.

14. **Act** Imagine the penguins in the photo decide to put on a performance on ice. Perform a dance routine or slapstick routine as if you were one of the penguins. Include the effects of Newton's first law in your routine.

Inertia and Newton's First Law

Newton's first law of motion is sometimes called the *law of inertia*. **Inertia** is the tendency of objects to resist any change in motion. Because of inertia, an object at rest will remain at rest unless a force makes it move. Likewise, inertia is the reason a moving object stays in motion with the same velocity unless a force changes its speed or direction.

15. Imagine that a passenger sets a phone on the dashboard of a car. There is little friction between the phone and the dashboard. The car moves at a constant velocity and then turns. What do you expect to happen to the phone when the car turns?

   A. The phone will stay in the same position relative to the dashboard and turn with the car because of friction.

   B. The phone will continue to move in a straight line because of inertia. The force of friction is not enough to change the motion of the phone.

   C. The phone will move in a straight line because a force is pushing the phone in a straight line.

   D. The phone will stay in the same position relative to the dashboard and turn with the car because of inertia.

Mass and Inertia

Objects with more mass have more inertia than objects with less mass. In fact, mass is a measure of inertia. More force is needed to overcome the inertia of a massive object to change its motion than is needed to cause the same change in the motion of a less massive object. Remember that an increase in velocity, a decrease in velocity, or a change of direction are all types of acceleration. Imagine how much force you need to pick up a bucket full of water compared to an empty bucket. You need more force because the full bucket has more inertia.

16. A person on a bicycle and a person driving a car are at rest at a stop light. The light turns green and both the cyclist and car begin to move. You would expect the *bicycle / car* to accelerate more quickly because the car has *less / more* mass than the bicycle, and thus *less / more* inertia.

EVIDENCE NOTEBOOK
17. How does Newton's first law apply to the motion of the golf tee that falls from the hoop into the bottle? Record your evidence.

Engineer It
Design Vehicles for Safety

Engineers study impacts that we might experience in a vehicle in order to improve our safety. Think about a bumper car collision and how it relates to a collision of a road vehicle. What additional safety equipment is available in a standard vehicle compared to a bumper car? Why do we have additional safety equipment in vehicles?

18. How does the airbag in the photo affect the motion of the driver in the car? Would this airbag protect the driver from a sideways collision? Explain your answer.

_____

_____

_____

_____

_____

Analyzing Newton's Second Law of Motion

We know from Newton's first law of motion that when an unbalanced force acts on an object, the object's motion changes. In other words, it accelerates. Newton's second. law describes the relationship between the acceleration and mass of an object when an unbalanced force is applied to the object.

The boy pushes a loaded cart down a school hallway.

The same loaded cart is now being pushed by two people.

19. How might the motion of the cart change when two people push the cart rather than when the boy pushes the cart by himself?

Newton's Second Law of Motion

Newton's second law of motion says that the acceleration of an object depends on the mass of the object and the amount of force applied. Notice that when talking about an applied force, this is the net force on an object. Only unbalanced forces will affect the acceleration of an object.

   To understand Newton's second law, consider the amount of force needed to accelerate two different masses. Think about the boy pushing the cart when it is loaded and when it is empty. If he wants the cart to accelerate at the same rate whether it is loaded or empty, how must he adjust the amount of force he uses to push the cart?

The boy pushes the same cart, but it is now empty.

20. When the cart is empty, it has *less / more* mass than when the cart is loaded. The boy must apply *less / more* force to the loaded cart for its acceleration to be the same as when it is empty.

You will explore the relationships among force, mass, and acceleration by investigating the motion of a cart. The cart's mass will be constant. You will increase the force applied to the cart and then measure the resulting acceleration of the cart using an accelerometer.

MATERIALS
- accelerometer
- cart, mass of at least 2 kg
- clamp
- hanger for masses
- pillow
- pulley with string
- slotted or hanging masses, each 100 g (4)
- video camera (optional)

Procedure

STEP 1 Set up the experiment as shown in the photo. The cart will be connected to a hanging mass by a string. The string passes over a pulley mounted at the edge of the table. A pillow will stop the hanging mass at the floor.

STEP 2 You will use the slotted or hanging masses hanging on the string to pull the cart with a constant amount of force. To determine the amount of force for the different masses, multiply the mass, in kilograms, by the acceleration due to gravity, 9.8 m/s². The result will be the force in newtons (N). Record your answers in a table like the one below.

Mass	Force (N)
100 g = 0.1 kg	0.98

STEP 3 Design a method to measure the acceleration of the cart when it is pulled by different amounts of force. Describe the method you will use.

STEP 4 Carry out your experiment.

STEP 5 Use the following table to convert the angle the string makes on the accelerometer (protractor) to acceleration.

Angle (degrees)	Acceleration (m/s^2)
0	0
5	0.86
10	1.7
15	2.6
20	3.5
25	4.6
30	5.7
35	6.9

STEP 6 Repeat Steps 4 and 5 with different amounts of force on the cart. On a separate sheet of paper, record the force and acceleration data in a table like the one shown below.

Force (N)	Acceleration (m/s^2)

Analysis

STEP 7 Graph the acceleration and force data on the axes. Graph the force on the x-axis and acceleration on the y-axis.

STEP 8 What relationship do you see between the acceleration and force when the mass of the cart is constant?

Express Newton's Second Law Mathematically

The relationship of force (F), mass (m), and acceleration (a) can be expressed mathematically with the equation $F = ma$, where force is in newtons (N), mass is in kilograms (kg), and acceleration is in meters per second per second (m/s^2). The table shows ways that this equation can be rearranged to calculate one of the variables when you know the other two.

Three Forms of Newton's Second Law		
I Want to Know	**I Know**	**Use This Equation**
acceleration (a)	mass (m) and force (F)	$a = F/m$
force (F)	mass (m) and acceleration (a)	$F = ma$
mass (m)	force (F) and acceleration (a)	$m = F/a$

21. Complete the table for the equation $a = F/m$, when $m = 1$ kg. Then graph the ordered pairs.

Force (N)	Acceleration (m/s²)
0	0
1	1
2	2
3	3

22. How does this graph compare to the data you graphed in the Hands-On Lab? How and why might they differ?

$$a = 1/1$$

Newton's Second Law of Motion and Friction

As you have seen, the acceleration of an object depends on the applied force. Imagine that you are pushing a loaded cart. You may notice that you must continue pushing on the cart to keep it moving at a constant velocity. Why does the cart not accelerate even though you are pushing on the cart? Friction. Recall that the force of friction opposes motion. In this case, your pushing force is balanced by the force of friction, so the net force on the cart is 0 N. The cart will continue to move at a constant velocity.

The Relationship between Acceleration, Mass, and Force

In the lab, you examined the relationship between acceleration and force. According to Newton's second law of motion, this relationship can be represented mathematically by the equation $a = F/m$. By looking at this equation and the experimental data, you can see that when force increases, the acceleration of an object with constant mass increases with the same multiplier as the force. This is why we say that an object's acceleration is *directly proportional* to the net force acting on the object.

Now, imagine that you are helping a library move. You are lifting boxes of books onto a cart. Most of the boxes are full of many books, but one of the boxes was closed only having a few books in it. You go to lift this box, not knowing it has less mass, with the same amount of force as you used to lift the full boxes. How will the acceleration of this box compare to the acceleration of a full box? Newton's second law of motion tells us that if the force remains constant and the mass is decreased, the object will accelerate at a faster rate. Because the acceleration increases when the mass decreases, we say that acceleration is *inversely proportional* to mass.

23. Give an example of a situation where you might use the mathematical formula for Newton's second law to solve a problem. Explain how the formula would be useful in this situation.

EVIDENCE NOTEBOOK

24. How does Newton's second law apply to the golf tee balanced on the hoop? How does Newton's second law apply to the golf tee when the hoop is pulled away? Record your evidence.

Engineer It
Relate Vehicle Mass to Performance

For a Formula One racecar, the ability to accelerate is critical to the car's performance. Much design effort is spent to create high-performance vehicles. How might the mass of a racecar affect its performance?

25. Engineers want a racecar to have as
    much / little mass as possible. A car
    with less mass requires less / more force
    to accelerate at the same rate as a car with
    more mass. So if two cars have the same
    engine, the car with less mass can accelerate
    less / more quickly than the car with
    more mass.

Engineers design racecars to accelerate quickly.

Analyzing Newton's Third Law of Motion

Newton's Third Law of Motion

Newton's third law of motion describes the forces involved when two objects interact. This law states that when one object applies a force to a second object, the second object applies an equal and opposite force to the first object.

26. Astronauts need special tools to work in space. One specially designed tool that astronauts use is a screwdriver. Using Newton's third law of motion, explain why it might be difficult to use a normal screwdriver to tighten a screw in space.

Astronauts must use special tools to work in space.

Action and Reaction Forces

The pair of forces described by Newton's third law are called *action and reaction forces*. Such action and reaction force pairs are present whenever two objects interact, even when there is no acceleration. For example, your body exerts a downward action force, your weight, on a chair when you sit on it. The upward reaction force, equal to your weight but in the opposite direction, is the force exerted by the chair on your body.

The action and reaction forces of a pair do not act on the same object. If they did, the net force would always be 0 N and nothing would ever accelerate! In the chair example, you are applying a force to the chair, and the chair is applying a force to you. The object you are analyzing determines which force is the action and which is the reaction. If you are interested in the person, the weight is the action force.

When you are identifying force pairs, it's important to know that action/reaction forces are always the same kind of force. For example, the reaction to a frictional force is a frictional force, and the reaction to a magnetic force is also a magnetic force.

This swimmer's feet push off against the wall of the pool, and the wall pushes back against the swimmer's feet.

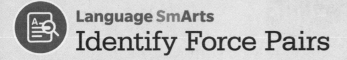
Identify Force Pairs

We rely on action and reaction force pairs when we interact with objects every day. When we apply forces to objects, the reaction force on our own body gives us information about the interaction.

A child attempts to hit a piñata with a stick.

27. **Draw** Imagine that the child is given earplugs in addition to being blindfolded so he cannot see or hear. Use Newton's third law to illustrate how he would know if he successfully hit the piñata. Include the appropriate force pairs and labels.

28. Describe the different action and reaction force pairs involved in the child hitting the piñata.

Newton's Second and Third Laws of Motion Combined

Gravity is a force of attraction between objects that is due to their masses. If you drop a ball, you know that gravity pulls the ball toward Earth. This force is the action force exerted by Earth's gravity on the ball. But gravity also pulls Earth toward the ball! This force is the reaction force exerted by the ball on Earth. It is easy to see the effect of the action force—the ball falling to Earth. Why do you not notice the effect of the reaction force—Earth being pulled upward?

Newton's third law tells us that when two objects interact, they experience equal but opposite forces. Newton's second law tells us that if the two objects have different masses, they will have different accelerations when acted on by the same force. Recall Newton's second law. In this example, the force applied to Earth is equal to the force applied to the ball. But the mass of Earth is much larger than the mass of the ball. Therefore, the acceleration of Earth due to this force is much smaller than the acceleration of the ball.

Action and reaction forces also occur when objects collide. Imagine walking around a corner in a hallway and bumping into someone much larger than you. What happens to your motion compared to the other person's motion? Think of other examples where two objects with different masses collide. How do Newton's laws of motion describe what happens after these collisions?

action force

reaction force

29. A particular bowling ball has a mass of 7 kg. A standard bowling pin has a mass of 1.5 kg. Use Newton's third law to describe what you expect to happen when the bowling ball collides with the pin. The ball applies an action force to the pin. The pin applies an equal action /reaction force to the ball. The forces in this force pair act in the same direction /opposite directions. Newton's second law tells us that the pin will accelerate more / less than the ball because it has less mass than the ball.

Apply Newton's Third Law

30. Ouch! Suppose you bumped your hand against the edge of a table. Use Newton's third law of motion to explain why your hand hurt.

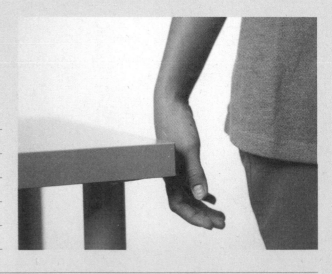

_____

_____

_____

_____

_____

_____

_____

Continue Your Exploration

Name: _____   Date: _____

Check out the path below or go online to choose one of the other paths shown.

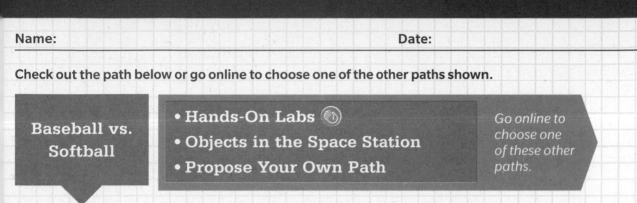

Baseball vs. Softball

- **Hands-On Labs** ✋
- **Objects in the Space Station**
- **Propose Your Own Path**

Go online to choose one of these other paths.

Baseball and softball are beloved games played all around the world. They share some obvious similarities, such as being played on a diamond and involving hitting a ball with a bat and running around the bases. However, compared to softballs, baseballs are lighter and smaller. They have a smaller circumference, which is the distance measured around the ball. Official game rules allow a narrow range of measurements, as shown below.

	Baseball	Softball
Mass	142 to 149 g (5 to $5\frac{1}{4}$ oz)	184 to 198 g ($6\frac{1}{2}$ to 7 oz)
Circumference	229 to 235 mm (9 to $9\frac{1}{4}$ in.)	302 to 311 mm ($11\frac{7}{8}$ to $12\frac{1}{4}$ in.)

When a bat hits a ball, some energy is transferred from the bat to the ball. In addition to this energy transfer, Newton's laws of motion can be used to analyze the motion of both the bat and the ball before, during, and after their collision.

This baseball player is about to hit the ball with a certain amount of force.

If this softball player hits the ball with the same amount of force as the baseball player, the ball will not go as far.

Continue Your Exploration

1. Use Newton's laws of motion to explain why it is important that baseballs and softballs each have a small acceptable range of masses.

2. Consider Newton's laws of motion. How would changing the mass of a bat affect a player's ability to swing the bat and adjust the path of the bat to hit a moving baseball or softball?

3. If a player swings a more massive bat at the same speed as a less massive bat, which bat would you expect to hit a baseball farther? Explain.

4. Consider all three of Newton's laws of motion. If a player swings the same bat at the same speed to hit a baseball and then a softball, which ball would you expect to go farther? Explain.

5. **Collaborate** Discuss with a partner whether you, as a baseball or softball player, would choose a more or less massive bat. Explain your reasoning.

Can You Explain It?

Name: Date:

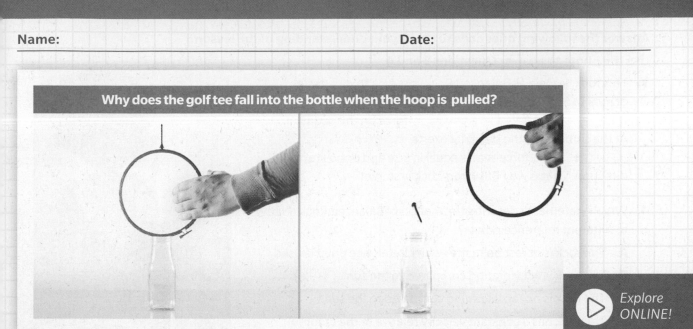

Why does the golf tee fall into the bottle when the hoop is pulled?

Explore ONLINE!

 EVIDENCE NOTEBOOK

Refer to the notes in your Evidence Notebook to help you construct an explanation for the motion of the golf tee.

1. State your claim. Make sure your claim fully explains why the golf tee falls into the bottle when the hoop is pulled.

2. Summarize the evidence you have gathered to support your claim and explain your reasoning.

Checkpoints

Answer the following questions to check your understanding of the lesson.

Use the photo to answer Questions 3 and 4.

3. This rock, known as Balanced Rock, sits on a thin pedestal of rock in a canyon in Idaho. Balanced Rock exerts *a downward / an upward* force on the pedestal. At the same time, the pedestal exerts *a downward / an upward* force that is equal in size and opposite in direction. That is why Balanced Rock is stable!

4. Which statements describe the motion of Balanced Rock relative to different reference points?

   A. The rock is at rest no matter which reference point is used.

   B. The rock is accelerating compared to the sun.

   C. The rock is not accelerating compared to the sun.

   D. The rock has a constant velocity relative to the moon.

Use the photo to answer Questions 5 and 6.

5. Imagine that the truck in the photo is acted on by an unbalanced force from the thrust of the air exiting the balloon. From the reference point of the truck, the balloon *is / is not* moving. The balloon *is / is not* moving from the reference point of the tape on the ground.

6. As the balloon pushes air backward, Newton's *first / second / third* law of motion states that the air will push the balloon forward. The balloon is attached to the truck, so the force on the balloon will also be applied to the truck. Newton's *first / second / third* law of motion states that this *balanced / unbalanced* force on the truck will cause the truck to move forward. Finally, Newton's *first / second / third* law of motion says that the acceleration of the truck will be proportional to the unbalanced force on the truck.

7. Given the position of an object at two different times, which of the following can you determine?

   A. The average speed of the object over the given time.

   B. The average velocity of the object over the given time.

   C. The average acceleration of the object over the given time.

Interactive Review

Complete this section to review the main concepts of the lesson.

Motion is a change in position over time relative to a reference point. Speed, velocity, and acceleration are used to describe the motion of objects.

A. How are speed, velocity, and acceleration related to each other?

Newton's first law says that an object at rest stays at rest and an object in motion stays in motion at the same speed and direction unless it experiences an unbalanced force.

B. What is inertia, and how does it relate to Newton's first law?

Newton's second law says that the acceleration of an object depends on the mass of the object and the amount of force applied.

C. What is the relationship between force, mass, and acceleration?

Newton's third law says that whenever one object exerts a force on a second object, the second object exerts an equal and opposite force on the first.

D. Create a model that shows an object interacting with another object. Show the forces and motion where appropriate.

Collisions between Objects

Percussionists use collisions to make music.

By the end of this lesson . . .

you will be able to apply Newton's laws of motion to design a solution to a problem involving two colliding objects.

CAN YOU EXPLAIN IT?

How can Newton's laws be applied to protect a smartphone screen during a collision?

People carry smartphones everywhere. If people are not careful, they can drop or bump their smartphones into other objects. Smartphones may be damaged in a collision.

1. Oh no! Have you ever seen this problem with a smartphone or a tablet? Write a step-by-step account of what you think might have happened to cause damage to the smartphone pictured.

 EVIDENCE NOTEBOOK As you work through the lesson, record evidence that helps you determine how to protect a smartphone screen during a collision.

Applying Newton's Laws to Collisions

Collisions between objects happen every day. A collision may be as simple as a ball bouncing on the ground. Other collisions, such as car crashes, may involve many objects and multiple collisions. These complex collisions may be more difficult to analyze than simple collisions. The motion of each object in a collision can be described by Newton's laws of motion.

2. **Discuss** Over the years, many meteoroids have collided with Earth. Many of these collisions occurred long ago, and the craters have been changed due to weathering. Look at the shape of Meteor Crater. What information does the crater's shape give you about the collision? What do you think happened to life in the area after the impact?

Meteor Crater in Arizona is one of the best preserved impact sites on Earth. The crater is almost 1 mile across and 240 feet deep. It was formed approximately 50,000 years ago.

Newton's Third Law of Motion and Collisions

When two objects collide, each object pushes the other. Think about hitting a softball with a bat. The bat collides with the ball and pushes it away. The ball also exerts a force on the bat. That is why you feel a stinging sensation in your hand as the bat vibrates.

Newton's third law states that when one object exerts a force on another, the second object exerts an equal but opposite force on the first object. These forces are sometimes called *action force* and *reaction force* or *force pairs*. These forces act only during the collision itself, which is often a very short period of time.

When the masses of two colliding objects are very different, the effect on the smaller object is greater than the effect on the larger one. When you hit the ball with the bat, the ball flies away but you and the bat do not. When a meteoroid strikes Earth, the force that the meteoroid exerts on Earth is the same strength as the force Earth exerts on the meteoroid. However, the effects are very different. Earth's crust gets a small dent, but the meteoroid is destroyed.

Newton's Second Law of Motion and Collisions

The robots are kicking identical balls; each kick is a collision. The effect of each kick on each ball depends on the ball's initial motion and the force of the kick. The force of the robot's kick causes the ball to accelerate. Remember that a change in the speed or direction of an object is acceleration. The robot is much more massive than the ball, so it accelerates less than the ball during the collision. This example illustrates Newton's second law of motion—the acceleration of an object depends on the mass of the object and the force applied to it (*F = ma*).

Robots Collide with Identical Balls

An object accelerates in the direction of the net force applied to it. The greater the force applied to the object, the greater the acceleration.

3. If the balls start at rest, the ball kicked with the most force will be moving <u>faster / slower</u> than the other balls after it is kicked. The ball with the greatest velocity will travel the <u>farthest / least</u> after it is kicked.
    The <u>yellow/red/blue</u> robot kicked with the most force. The evidence is the <u>distance the ball traveled/size of the robot</u>.

4. **Draw** A satellite collides with debris in space. Draw a picture showing the collision. Show the forces and indicate their likely effects.

Newton's First Law of Motion and Collisions

Different objects behave differently during collisions. Many objects actually deform, or change shape, during a collision. Cars are designed to deform in specific ways during a collision. This is an important safety feature because it reduces the force acting on the passengers in the car. Some of the energy from the moving car goes into deforming the vehicle rather than affecting the passengers.

Recall that Newton's first law of motion describes the inertia of an object, or an object's resistance to a change in motion. How does inertia affect collisions? Look at the car crash shown. You know that when the car stops, the passengers will continue to move due to inertia. This is why we have seat belts to stop passengers during a collision. How does inertia explain the crumpling of the car during the collision?

Automotive engineers study collisions to protect passengers from harm in collisions such as this one.

5. **Collaborate** With a partner, analyze the collision shown in the photo. Use your knowledge of Newton's laws of motion and collisions to describe the motion of the car throughout the collision.

Simple Collisions

In a simple collision, deformations and energy losses are not considered. A simple collision can be analyzed using Newton's laws of motion. Analyzing simple collisions can help engineers and scientists explain more complex collisions, such as a car crash. Let's look at some examples of simple collisions to see how the masses of the objects in a collision affect the objects' motions before, during, and after a collision. As you think about the following examples, consider how each of Newton's laws of motion can be applied to each situation.

Collisions between Objects with Equal Masses

Consider the two marbles shown in the image. Both marbles have the same mass. Before the collision, the blue marble is moving from left to right. The orange marble is at rest. From Newton's first law, we know that the blue marble will continue to move, and the orange marble will stay at rest—until they collide, that is. When the marbles collide, Newton's third law tells us that the force each exerts on the other is equal in strength and opposite in direction. Because the masses are the same, Newton's second law tells us that the acceleration of the balls during the collision will also be equal and opposite. The blue marble accelerates in the direction of the force exerted on the blue marble. In this example, this acceleration is in the opposite direction of the marble's original velocity. So the blue marble's speed will decrease. One possible result of this collision would be that the blue marble stops moving and the orange marble begins moving to the right at the same speed the blue marble initially had.

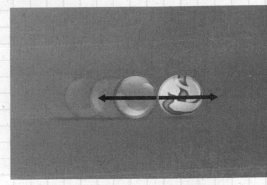

During the collision, each marble exerts a force on the other marble. This force pair is shown in the image.

6. Explain how the collision would or would not change if both marbles were moving before the collision, instead of only the blue marble moving. Use Newton's laws of motion to support your reasoning.

Collisions between Objects with Different Masses

Many collisions involve objects with different masses. We know that each ball in the collision shown will experience an equal and opposite force. From Newton's second law, we know that the acceleration of an object depends on its mass and the applied force. How will that relationship affect a collision between two objects with different masses?

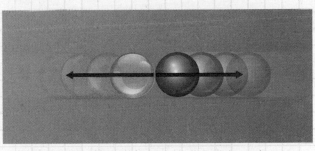

A glass marble collides with a steel ball. Both have the same dimensions, but the steel ball has a greater mass.

7. Which of the statements are true about the collision of two objects with different masses based on Newton's laws of motion?

   A. Each object experiences an equal and opposite force.

   B. The more massive object will exert a greater force on the less massive object.

   C. Each object will accelerate in an opposite direction from the other but at a different rate.

   D. The less massive object will accelerate due to the force of the collision, but the more massive object will not.

Analyze Acceleration During a Collision

Before the collision, the two marbles shown are moving at equal speeds in opposite directions. Both marbles have the same mass. When two objects with the same mass collide, Newton's laws tell us that they will accelerate the same amount but in opposite directions. Recall that force, velocity, and acceleration have both magnitude and direction. We use positive and negative signs to indicate the direction of each of these quantities.

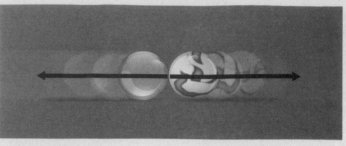

Notice that the force arrows on each marble are equal in magnitude and opposite in direction.

8. Before the collision, the blue marble is moving from left to right, and it has a velocity of 2 m/s. The orange marble is moving at an equal speed but in the opposite direction. What is the velocity of the orange marble before the collision?

9. During the collision, both marbles accelerate to a stop, or 0 m/s. Use the formula $V_{final} - V_{initial}$ to calculate the change in velocities for the orange and blue marbles.

    Orange marble: 0 m/s – (–2 m/s) = 2 m/s

    Blue marble: 0 m/s – 2 m/s = ▢

10. What can you say about the change in velocities of the marbles?

11. The velocities of the marbles change, so we know that the marbles accelerate. Acceleration is the rate of change of velocity, which is the change in velocity divided by time. To calculate acceleration during a collision, the time is the duration of the collision, which is the same for both objects in the collision. What can you say about the accelerations of the blue and orange marbles during this collision?

12. Use Newton's laws of motion to write a description of the motion of both marbles during this collision.

Collisions with Objects in Contact

What happens when an object collides with a second identical object that is touching a third identical object? The object in the middle effectively transfers the force of the collision to the third object. The third object will then move as a result of the collision, but the second object will not move. When the balls are moving, they have *kinetic energy*. This energy is transferred to the other balls during each collision. During each transfer, there are some losses as the energy is transformed into other types of energy such as sound energy and thermal energy. You can hear a clicking sound during each collision as evidence of these losses.

The Newton's cradle is an example of how collisions work when objects are in contact.

13. **Language SmArts** Based on Newton's laws of motion, you might expect that once the Newton's cradle is set in motion, it will stay in motion forever. Make an argument about whether this is true or not. Support your claim with evidence.

EVIDENCE NOTEBOOK

14. Why might a smartphone be damaged when it falls on a hard surface? Record your evidence.

Analyze a Bocce Shot

In the game of bocce, two teams roll their balls toward a target ball. The goal of the game is to have the ball that is the closest to the target ball after each team throws their balls.

15. The blue team is rolling one of their balls toward another of their balls, which is touching an opponent's ball as shown. What do you predict will happen when the balls collide? Will this be a good shot for the blue team?

_____

_____

_____

_____

Engineering a Solution to a Collision Problem

Effects of Collisions

You know from experience that collisions have different effects depending on the objects involved and the motion of the objects just before the collision. A soccer ball has a greater acceleration when it is kicked with a greater force than when it is kicked with a lower force. If a ball is moving toward a player, a kick will have a different effect than if the ball is not moving. A tennis ball bounces differently on a clay surface compared to a grass surface or a hard surface.

16. The bird flies over different surfaces. How will the surface onto which the bird drops the clam affect whether the clam will open?

A bird drops a clam to break the shell open for food.

The bird uses a collision to its advantage. Humans also use collisions to achieve a goal, such as hammering a nail. Unfortunately, not all effects of collisions are desirable; they can be dangerous or damaging. Imagine the hammer hitting your thumb instead of the nail. Ouch! Because damaging collisions will happen sometimes, engineers work to develop solutions to reduce the damage caused by collisions.

17. **Draw** Imagine a stunt person falling onto an airbag. The airbag is designed to slowly bring the stunt person to a rest. Imagine this collision in slow motion. Draw a series of three images showing the motion of the stunt person at the beginning, middle, and end of the collision with the airbag.

18. **Discuss** With a partner, discuss how the motion of the stunt person relates to the forces acting on the stunt person during the collision.

Hands-On Lab
Test Packing Materials

Packaging designers need data on packing materials in order to choose the best materials to meet their needs. Test engineers design tests to collect this data. In this lab, you will design a testing method and perform tests on different packing materials. A successful testing method is repeatable and will give engineers the data they need to choose the best materials for their packing needs.

Procedure and Analysis

STEP 1 The list below is an incomplete list of criteria and constraints for this engineering design problem. With your group, discuss the engineering problem and add at least one constraint and one criterion to better define the problem.

Criteria	Constraints
Testing method can be used to test a variety of materials.	Testing method can be performed with materials available in the classroom
	Testing can be completed within one class period.

STEP 2 Brainstorm ideas for testing methods that can be used to evaluate the effectiveness of different packing materials. Do not evaluate the ideas yet. Record each idea in a notebook.

STEP 3 Choose a method from Step 2 that you will implement. Draw or describe the method, and explain why it is the most promising solution. Show your method and explanation to your teacher.

STEP 4 Implement your chosen testing method, and record the test results for each of the packing materials being tested.

Students examine their egg after a test.

STEP 5 Does your testing method satisfy your criteria and constraints? Describe how you might improve your testing method.

STEP 6 Based on your testing, what qualities make a material useful for protecting an item during a collision?

Energy and Collisions

Objects and systems may contain different amounts and types of energy. When an object is moving, it has kinetic energy. What happens to this energy during a collision? Some of the energy remains with the object. Some of the energy is transferred from one object to the other during the collision. Some of the energy is transformed into other forms such as sound energy or thermal energy. If an object in a collision is made of an elastic material, the energy may temporarily be stored as *elastic potential energy* as the object deforms. When the object returns to its original shape, this elastic potential energy transforms back into kinetic energy. Whenever energy is transformed into another form, some of the energy is lost. These losses may be desirable depending on the situation. For example, when a percussionist hits a drum, some of the energy is transformed into sound energy and is lost from the system. While Newton's laws of motion can be used to describe the motion of objects during a collision, sometimes other concepts are needed to fully analyze a collision.

 19. Language SmArts The image shows a tennis ball during a collision with the ground. Explain in detail why the tennis ball bounces. Use Newton's laws of motion and information from the text to support your reasoning.

Explore ONLINE!

A tennis ball deforms as it bounces on the ground.

 EVIDENCE NOTEBOOK

20. How can the lab results help you design protection for a smartphone screen during a collision? Record your evidence.

Do the Math | Analyze the Effect of Collision Duration on Acceleration

When objects collide, the duration of the collision is measured from the time of initial contact to the time when the objects are no longer in contact or when they have stopped accelerating relative to each other. If an object deforms during a collision, the duration of the collision is extended. Do the math to see how changing the duration of a collision affects the magnitude of the acceleration.

21. Objects A and B, each with a mass of 20 kg, collide with a much larger object. Both A and B have a velocity of 10 m/s just before the collision and come to a full stop after the collision. The duration of the collision of object A is 0.001 s. The duration of the collision of object B is 0.002 s. Calculate the acceleration of each object using the formula $a = (V_{final} - V_{initial})/t$.

Object A $\qquad \dfrac{0 \text{ m/s} - 10 \text{ m/s}}{0.001 \text{ s}} = \dfrac{-10 \text{ m/s}}{0.001 \text{ s}} = -10{,}000 \text{ m/s}^2$

Object B $\qquad \dfrac{0 \text{ m/s} - 10 \text{ m/s}}{\boxed{} \text{ s}} = \dfrac{-10 \text{ m/s}}{\boxed{} \text{ s}} = \boxed{} \text{ m/s}^2$

22. Use the accelerations of objects A and B to explain how a collision's duration affects the object's acceleration.

Design Packaging

Packages are shipped all over the world. Often what is being shipped needs to be protected from collisions that occur during shipping. Consumers and companies desire minimal packaging to minimize waste and package weight, but the product must be protected.

23. Explain how you would begin designing a solution to the problem of protecting a fragile item, such as a laptop, during shipping.

A drone delivers a package.

Continue Your Exploration

Name: _____   Date: _____

Check out the path below or go online to choose one of the other paths shown.

Careers in Engineering

- **Wrecking Ball Demolitions**
- **Propose Your Own Path**

Go online to choose one of these other paths.

Crash Test Engineer

You have probably seen videos of crash test dummies in a car collision. Crash test engineers design ways to test the effects of a car collision on a car's passengers and to improve car designs to be safer. Recording devices on crash test dummies measure forces experienced by the bodies during a collision. Engineers then analyze this data and use it to design better safety devices for vehicles. Safety measures include devices such as safety belts and airbags, which apply forces directly to passengers to protect them. Car bodies themselves are engineered to deform in specific places to protect the passengers. A crash test engineer often has a degree in mechanical engineering or industrial engineering. The job requires an understanding of physics, math, and how to use computers to analyze data.

A crash test is performed with a cyclist colliding with the side of a car. Video and sensors on the crash test dummies record data about the acceleration and forces experienced by the crash test dummies.

Continue Your Exploration

1. Based on the description of a crash test engineer's job, which of these engineering tasks would the engineer work on? Choose all that apply.

   A. testing prototypes of a new design to determine whether they meet safety criteria

   B. choosing materials used in automobile manufacturing

   C. studying customer preferences to improve marketing

   D. using a computer to analyze large amounts of data

2. Which of the following may affect a passenger's safety during a collision?

   A. the mass of the automobile in which the passenger rides

   B. the mass of the automobile that collides with the passenger's vehicle

   C. the velocity of the passenger's vehicle

   D. the acceleration of the passenger's vehicle during the collision

3. Automobiles did not always have safety devices such as safety belts, airbags, and roll cages. What societal needs led to the creation of these safety measures and the career of crash test engineering?

4. **Collaborate** Work with a partner or a group. Consider the engineering design process involved in making cars and trucks. Make a list of other jobs in the automotive industry that could also be filled by mechanical or industrial engineers.

Can You Explain It?

Name: _____ **Date:** _____

How can Newton's laws be applied to protect a smartphone screen during a collision?

EVIDENCE NOTEBOOK

Refer to the notes in your Evidence Notebook to help you construct an explanation for how to protect a smartphone screen during a collision.

1. State your claim. Make sure your claim fully explains how a smartphone can be protected during a collision.

2. Summarize the evidence you have gathered to support your claim.

Checkpoints

Answer the following questions to check your understanding of the lesson.

Use the photo to answer Questions 3 and 4.

3. The mat in the photo helps protect the gymnast by decreasing / increasing the duration of the collision between the gymnast and the floor. Decreasing / Increasing the duration of the collision decreases the acceleration / velocity of the gymnast during the collision.

4. Which of the following criteria are satisfied by the mat in the photo?

    A. does not interfere with gymnast during a routine on the rings

    B. is easily transported by a single person

    C. protects a gymnast from injury during a dismount from the rings

    D. fits in a small car

Use the photo to answer Question 5.

5. The photo shows evidence of meteors colliding with the moon. According to Newton's laws, what can be said about these collisions?

    A. During each collision, the moon exerted a greater force on each meteor than each meteor exerted on the moon.

    B. The moon and meteors exerted equal but opposite forces on the each other.

    C. The collisions were so small that no forces acted on either the moon or the meteors during the collisions.

    D. Because the moon has no atmosphere, Newton's laws cannot be applied to the collisions between the moon and meteors.

6. In a simple collision between two objects, Newton's laws of motion can be used to describe the motion of which of the objects?

    A. Both objects

    B. Only objects that are moving before the collision

    C. Neither object

Interactive Review

Complete this section to review the main concepts of the lesson.

Newton's laws of motion can be used to describe the motions of objects involved in a collision.

A. How can Newton's laws of motion be used to analyze the collision between two objects?

The engineering design process can be used to develop a solution to an engineering problem, including a problem of objects colliding.

B. Collisions may cause unwanted damage to an object. Describe how the engineering design process can be used to design a solution to protect an object during a collision.

Choose one of the activities to explore how this unit connects to other topics.

☐ Earth Science Connection

Erupting Evidence Earth's crust is broken into large fragments known as tectonic plates. When tectonic plates collide, slide past one another, or separate, earthquakes, tsunamis, volcanoes, or the formation of mountains can occur on the surface of Earth.

Research how the movement of tectonic plates affects geology, and explain how scientists measure the forces caused by these movements. Make a multimedia presentation to share what you learn with your class.

☐ Technology Connection

Gravity in Space Objects and astronauts have the same amount of mass on the International Space Station as on Earth, but they seem to be weightless because everything is in *free fall*, which means it is all falling toward Earth at the same rate. This allows astronauts to conduct experiments on the effects of these, conditions on organisms and objects. Special tools have been developed to work in free fall, such as the space pen.

Research a technology or experiment that has been developed to work in free-fall conditions. Create a diagram or model demonstrating how forces are used to make the apparatus or procedure work.

☐ Art Connection

Kinetic Sculpture Kinetic art refers to a sculpture or other artwork that moves, often from the forces of wind, a motor, or a person interacting with the object. The American artist Alexander Calder developed the first mobiles, hanging sculptures with individual moving parts that gracefully rotate in a breeze.

Create your own piece of kinetic art and explain how its motion is caused by the forces acting on it. Or, select an interesting piece of kinetic art and research the background of its production and the artist who designed it. Make a diagram illustrating the forces that cause movement in the piece of art.

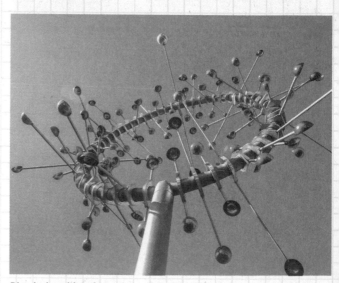

Blowhole, a kinetic sculpture designed by Duncan Stemler for Docklands Park in Melbourne, Australia.

Name: _____   Date: _____

Complete this review to check your understanding of the unit.

Use the image of the hovercraft to answer Questions 1–3.

1. A hovercraft uses blowers to force air underneath it, allowing it to coast on a thin layer of air above the ground or water. What type of force is it reducing?

   A. gravity

   B. speed

   C. friction

   D. acceleration

2. Calculate the acceleration of the craft if the mass of a person on the hovercraft is 68 kg and the amount of force acting on the person due to acceleration is 408 Newtons.

   A. 6 m/s^2

   B. 68 m/s^2

   C. 340 m/s^2

   D. 476 m/s^2

This hovercraft coasts on a thin layer of air over land or water. The propeller on the back of the craft propels the hovercraft forward.

3. How much additional force would the craft have to exert to achieve the same acceleration if another 52 kg person got onboard the craft?

   A. no additional force is necessary

   B. 8 newtons

   C. 96 newtons

   D. 312 newtons

Use the line graph to answer Questions 4 and 5.

4. What type of motion does line B represent?

   A. an object moving at a constant speed

   B. an object at rest

   C. an object moving at an increasing speed

   D. an object moving at a decreasing speed

5. What kind of object could be represented by line C?

   A. a bird landing in sand

   B. a car accelerating away

   C. a car coming to a sudden stop

   D. a horse slowing from a trot to a walk

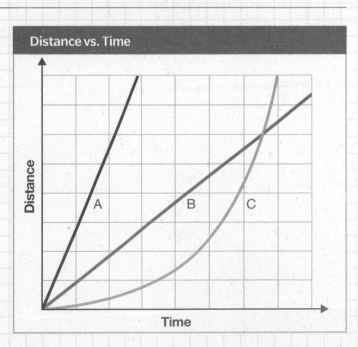

Distance vs. Time

Distance

A   B   C

Time

6. Fill in the graphic organizer to show how each phenomenon of force and motion relates to each of the big-picture concepts.

Phenomenon	Stability and Change	Cause and Effect	Real-world Examples
Acceleration	Acceleration represents a change in velocity.		
Friction			
Gravity			
Collisions			

Name: _____   Date: _____

Use the image to answer Questions 7–10.

7. Two people wearing inflatable bubble suits collide with one another while playing soccer. Describe the contact and noncontact forces acting on the players.

8. Person A has a mass of 100 kg and Person B has a mass of 50 kg. They are both moving at the same speed toward one another. What will happen when they collide?

9. If both people had the same mass and were moving at the same speed when they collided, what would happen?

10. Use the example of the two soccer players in the ball suits to explain Newton's third law.

Use the image to answer Questions 11–13.

11. Why does a hockey puck move more easily on ice than on cement?

12. Create a force diagram modeling the forces acting between a hockey stick and a puck.

13. What examples of inertia (the tendency of an object to resist a change in motion) can be observed during a game of ice hockey?

Name: _____ **Date:** _____

Can you improve the design of a toy hoop?

You work for a toy design company that is trying to update the classic toy hoop. Your boss wants you to explain how a toy hoop stays around a person's waist or arm. Based on your research, she wants you to improve the company's toy hoop design so a person can more easily keep it in motion for a longer period of time. Develop a procedure to accurately test how a change in the mass or size of a toy hoop changes the object's motion. Then prepare a presentation of your findings for your boss.

The steps below will help guide your research to develop your recommendation.

Engineer It

1. **Ask a Question** Develop a statement clearly defining the problem you have been asked to solve. What questions will you need to answer to explain how a toy hoop stays around a person's waist or arm?

Engineer It

2. Conduct Research Research the forces acting on a toy hoop that allow it to stay around a person's waist or arm. Investigate the average size and mass of a toy hoop.

3. Plan an Investigation Plan a procedure to determine how changes in the mass or size of a toy hoop change its motion. Conduct several trials with different design prototypes for comparison.

4. Construct an Explanation Explain your test results. Use this data to suggest a recommendation for improving the design of the toy hoop.

5. Communicate Prepare a presentation describing your findings for the boss of the toy company. Include evidence from your test results to support your argument.

 **Self-Check**

	I asked questions about how toy hoops stay in motion and how changes in mass change an object's motion.
	I researched the forces acting on toy hoops and the average mass and size of a standard toy hoop.
	I planned an investigation to test how changes in the mass or size of a toy hoop affect its motion.
	I prepared a presentation describing my findings and recommended an improved design based on evidence from my test results.

Electric and Magnetic Forces

During thunderstorms, electric charges build up within clouds to produce spectacular lightning displays.

Electric and magnetic forces surround us here on Earth. Earth itself is a giant magnet, and upper layers of the atmosphere are filled with electrically charged particles. Electric and magnetic forces are involved in technologies used for communication, medicine, and transportation, and they power devices from lamps to smartphones. In this unit, you will investigate electric and magnetic forces and the very close relationship between them.

Why It Matters

Here are some questions to consider as you work through the unit. Can you answer any of the questions now? Revisit these questions at the end of the unit to apply what you discover.

Questions	Notes
Where have you seen electric and magnetic forces in everyday life?	
What features do electric and magnetic forces have in common?	
How are electromagnetic forces used to generate electric power?	
How could you measure the force generated by a charged object?	
What applications do electric and magnetic forces have in transportation?	
What other problems can be solved by applying knowledge of electric and magnetic forces?	

Unit Starter: Identifying Effects of Magnetic Forces

Magnets produce a force that pushes or pulls on other magnets. Think of times you have experimented with magnets. You may recall that magnets have north and south poles and that these poles affect how magnets interact with each other. The images below show a "before" and "after" effect on a magnet. Study the images and answer the questions below.

before

after

1. Which of the following is the best explanation for what is taking place in the "before" and "after" images?

   A. An attractive force between the magnets pulls them together.

   B. An attractive force between the magnets pushes them apart.

   C. A repulsive force between the magnets pulls them together.

   D. A repulsive force between the magnets pushes them apart.

2. How must the magnets be related in order for this interaction to occur?

   A. The "opposite" poles of the magnets must be next to each other.

   B. The "like" poles of the magnets must be next to each other.

   C. The orientation of the magnetic poles does not matter.

   D. The two magnets must be the same size.

Go online to download the Unit Project Worksheet to help you plan your project.

Unit Project

Electric Charge Detector

Do you have a doorbell or a buzzer where you live? Have you ever wondered how it works? Now is your chance to design, build, and test your own alert system using an electromagnet.

Magnetic Forces

Magnets are able to attract or repel certain materials, such as iron, at a distance.

By the end of this lesson . . .

you will be able to describe the variables that affect the strength and direction of the magnetic force.

CAN YOU EXPLAIN IT?

Why do these rings seem to float without touching one another instead of falling?

If you were to drop one of these rings onto a peg, you would normally expect it to fall and hit another ring. Instead, when the rings get near one another, they are pushed back up and appear to float.

Explore ONLINE!

1. Most objects are not able to float in midair. What must be occurring for these rings to float instead of fall?

2. What type of force might be affecting the motion of these rings?

 EVIDENCE NOTEBOOK As you explore the lesson, gather evidence to help explain the behavior of the rings.

Describing Magnets and the Magnetic Force

A **magnet** is an object that attracts, or pulls on, materials that contain iron. Other materials, such as cobalt and nickel, are also attracted to magnets. Magnets can attract and repel, or push away, other magnets. All magnets have a north pole and a south pole. These poles affect how magnets interact with each other. Look at the photos and notice how the magnets affect each other, even though they are not touching.

3. Why do you think that these two magnets are able to affect one another's movements even when they are not touching?

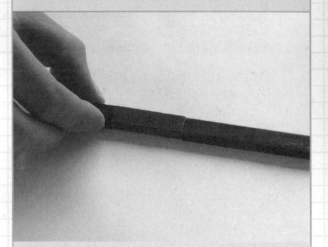

Magnet Interactions

▶ Explore ONLINE!

The north and south poles of the magnets in this image are different colors. The north pole has been painted red and the south pole has been painted gray. Every magnet has a north and a south pole.

When these magnets are brought close enough together, they will jump toward one another. The two magnets affect each other's movement even though they were not originally touching.

The **magnetic force** is the push or pull exerted by magnets. As you can see in the photos, this force acts at a distance. Like all forces, the strength of magnetic force varies in predictable ways. However, even very strong magnets only attract and/or repel certain materials.

 EVIDENCE NOTEBOOK

4. How might the ability of magnets to attract or repel other magnets relate to the floating rings? Record your evidence.

Hands-On Lab
Explore the Behavior of Magnets

You will ask questions to investigate the behavior of magnets and then you will explore how magnets affect a variety of materials and identify the factors that affect the strength of the magnetic force.

Procedure

STEP 1 Below are a few questions to consider as you explore the factors that affect the strength of the magnetic force. Write at least two more questions you could investigate using the materials.

- How do the magnets affect materials that are not magnets?
- How does the force between the two bar magnets compare to the force between the other magnet and a bar magnet?
- How do the poles of the magnets affect the force they exert on each other?

STEP 2 Choose two questions to investigate. Identify the variables you will be testing for each investigation. Revise your questions if needed so your investigation will help you determine whether there is a relationship between the variables, and if so, what that relationship is. On a separate sheet of paper, write your procedure for each question and record your observations.

Analysis

STEP 3 **Discuss** With a partner, compare your observations. Using your combined observations, decide on the factors that seemed to affect the strength of the magnetic force. Record your answers below.

STEP 4 The magnetic force is attractive / repulsive when two like poles point toward each other. The magnetic force is attractive / repulsive when two opposite poles point toward each other. When the like poles of two magnets point toward one another, the strength of the magnetic force is the same as when the opposite poles point toward one another.

Hands-On Lab
Analyze the Magnetic Force

Part 1: Distance and the Magnetic Force

You will investigate the relationship between distance and the strength of the magnetic force using a magnet and a compass. The needle of a compass is magnetic and points north due to Earth's magnetic field. If the attractive force between the compass needle and a magnet is strong enough, the compass needle will move toward the magnet.

   The distance between two magnets affects the strength of the magnetic force. When two magnets are moved closer together, the magnetic force between them increases. When two magnets are moved farther apart, the magnetic force between them decreases.

MATERIALS
- bar magnet
- compass
- tape
- tape measure or ruler

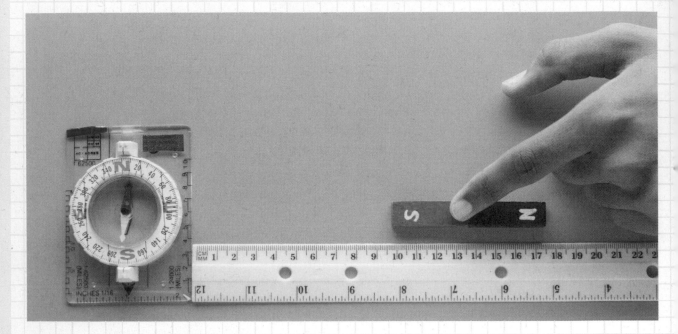

Procedure and Analysis

STEP 1 Tape your compass to the table so that the needle points directly toward one of the sides of the compass. Record the direction in degrees that the compass needle is pointing.

STEP 2 Place the bar magnet so that the south pole of the magnet is pointed toward the compass. It should be far enough away that it does not affect the needle. The needle and the magnet should be perpendicular to one another.

STEP 3 Move the magnet straight toward the compass until the needle moves 15° from its starting position. Record the distance between the edge of the bar magnet closest to the compass and the edge of the compass.

STEP 4 Move the magnet four more times, recording the distance and the position of the needle in degrees. Choose increments so that your last data point is collected with the magnet touching the compass.

STEP 5 Record the number of degrees the needle moved from its starting position for each distance, or measured position.

STEP 6 **Do the Math** Make a graph of your data with degrees on the y-axis and distance on the x-axis. Graphs can help you clearly see the relationship between variables in an experiment.

Distance (cm)	Needle Position (degrees)

STEP 7 Look at the trend shown in your graph. Consider how the strength of the magnetic force relates to the needle position. What effect does distance seem to have on the strength of the magnetic force?

Part 2: Magnet Strength and the Magnetic Force

MATERIALS
- magnet, bar
- magnet, large
- paper clips, metal (10)
- mass set, hooked (10 g–1 kg)

You will test the strength of the magnetic forces produced by two magnets by comparing the masses that they can hold.

The strength of the magnetic force exerted by a magnet depends on the magnet. Some magnets produce a stronger magnetic force than others. The material and size of a magnet affect the strength of the magnetic force.

Procedure and Analysis

STEP 1 Hook each mass to a paper clip.

STEP 2 Hang the end of the paper clip with the lightest mass from the bar magnet. Remove the paper clip and mass.

STEP 3 Repeat Step 2 with the other paper clips and masses, gradually increasing the mass, until the magnet can no longer hold the paper clip.

STEP 4 Consider how you could make your measurements more accurate using your supplies. If you had a magnet that could hold a maximum of 150 g, but did not have a 150 g mass, how could you measure this? Develop a process to measure the maximum mass that each magnet can hold.

STEP 5 Repeat Steps 2–4 with the large magnet.

STEP 6 **Language SmArts** Record your observations. Write a claim that states how you believe the type of magnet affects the strength of the magnetic force. Use evidence from your observations to support your claim, and explain your reasoning. You can also draw on information about the magnetic force that you learned before this investigation.

STEP 7 Based on your observations, what can you infer about the strength of the magnets based on the magnetic force that they exert?

A. The strength of the bar magnet is greater than the strength of the larger magnet because the bar magnet produces a weaker magnetic force.

B. The strength of the bar magnet is less than the strength of the larger magnet because the bar magnet produces a weaker magnetic force.

C. The strength of the bar magnet is greater than the strength of the larger magnet because the bar magnet produces a stronger magnetic force.

D. The strength of the bar magnet is less than the strength of the larger magnet because the bar magnet produces a stronger magnetic force.

EVIDENCE NOTEBOOK

5. Do distance and the strength of different magnets seem to affect the behavior of the rings? If so, how can the these variables be related to the forces acting on the rings? Record your evidence.

Analyze How Magnets Are Used

Magnets exert a magnetic force that can pull on certain materials. Depending on whether the like or opposite poles are facing each other, magnets push or pull on other magnets. A magnetic force often is used to hold together objects, such as magnetic clasp on a bag or a refrigerator magnet. A magnetic force can also be used to push apart objects. Maglev trains can travel at very high speeds because they use magnetic force to float, or levitate, above the tracks.

A maglev train does not have wheels that roll on the tracks. Instead, the train uses a strong magnetic force to levitate, eliminating friction.

6. The magnetic force pushing the train away from the tracks is strong enough to overcome the force of gravity, allowing the train to levitate. If the poles of the magnets on the train were reversed, what would happen to the train?

Exploring Why Materials Are Magnetic

Magnets display properties that are unique to a select group of materials. While iron displays magnetism, other metals such as copper aren't attracted to magnets in the same way. There is something fundamentally different about the properties of materials that generate a magnetic force and are attracted to magnets.

7. When a magnet is cut in half, both halves become magnets with north and south poles. Why do you think magnets always have north and south poles, even after they are cut in half?

Atoms and Magnets

The magnetic properties of a material are a result of the overall magnetic properties of its atoms. Many atoms and molecules generate very small magnetic forces. Some atoms, such as iron, produce a stronger magnetic force than other atoms. These atoms can be thought of as tiny magnets, with a north and south each pole. If the poles are oriented in all directions, the material will not produce a net magnetic force. Due to these randomly oriented magnetic forces, most materials are not magnetic.

8. In a small iron particle made of 200 atoms, the north poles of 100 atoms are pointed right and the north poles of another 100 atoms are pointed left. Which statement describes the net magnetic force exerted by the iron particle?

   A. The net magnetic force is about zero.

   B. The net magnetic force is less than zero.

   C. The net magnetic force is 100 times as strong as the force of the atoms.

   D. The net magnetic force is 200 times as strong as the force of the atoms.

The atoms in this material are represented as magnets with north and south poles. Notice that poles point in many different directions. As a result, the tiny magnetic forces average to nearly zero, producing no overall magnetic force.

Magnetic Domains

In some materials, such as iron, the north poles of groups of atoms can line up in the same direction in areas called **magnetic domains**. Within each domain, the like poles of the atoms point in the same direction, so their magnetic fields are also aligned in the same direction. However, the poles of atoms in one domain may point in a different direction than the poles of atoms in another domain. Materials that form magnetic domains are called *ferromagnetic materials*. Iron, nickel, and cobalt are all examples of ferromagnetic materials.

Magnetic Domain Alignment

Materials that are attracted to magnets, such as iron, can have magnetic domains. However, the domains normally point in random directions. Because the sum of the magnetic forces of the different domains is either zero or very small, iron does not normally exert a magnetic force on other objects.

When a material with magnetic domains is exposed to a magnetic force, the domains realign themselves. The magnetic domains become aligned and the material temporarily becomes a magnet. This realignment causes iron to be attracted to magnets. Permanent magnets generate a net magnetic force because their magnetic domains always remain aligned.

9. Iron nails are attracted to magnets, but they are not attracted to each other. Explain why iron nails may behave this way.

10. Draw In the space on the right, sketch how the magnetic domains of two iron nails might appear when they are near each other. Next, sketch how the magnetic domains of an iron nail might appear when placed near the north pole of a magnet. Use arrows to show the alignment of the magnetic domains, with the arrowhead representing the north pole.

EVIDENCE NOTEBOOK

11. What kind of force did the levitating rings display? What does this say about the magnetic domains of these objects? Record your evidence.

Engineer It Though we know magnetic domains exist, they are not visible to the human eye. In addition to being very small, the domains are not visible under normal circumstances. However, a special method can be used to visualize them. The Kerr microscope makes use of the fact that the magnetic force affects light in subtle ways.

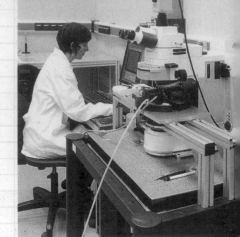

The Kerr microscope first shines light through a filter. The light then bounces off of the magnetic material and is changed slightly by the magnetic force. The light then passes through another filter. Due to this filter system, the change in the light due to the material's magnetism can be seen with the microscope.

In order to understand how a technology such as this could be developed, identify which statement matches the following steps of the engineering design process. Not every item in the word bank will be used.

12. Scientists are unable to visualize the magnetism of materials.

_____

13. Scientists discover that the magnetic strength of a material can affect how light interacts with the material.

_____

14. A microscope designed to measure how light changes after it reflects off of a magnetic object is run through several trials to test if it works correctly.

_____

> **WORD BANK**
> - defining engineering problems
> - developing solutions
> - testing solutions
> - optimizing solutions

Analyze Temporary Magnets

A magnetic domain is a group of atoms with their poles aligned in the same direction. In permanent magnets, the magnetic domains are aligned with each other to produce a net magnetic force. Some materials can become temporary magnets. This iron screwdriver temporarily became magnetic after it was exposed to a strong magnet.

15. How did the screwdriver become temporarily magnetic?

 A. Magnetic domains formed in the metal of the screwdriver when it was exposed to the magnet.

 B. The magnetic domains in the screwdriver were temporarily aligned by the presence of the magnet.

 C. The force exerted by the screws made the magnetic domains in the metal of the screwdriver line up.

 D. The magnet erased the magnetic domains in the screwdriver.

Continue Your Exploration

Name: _____   Date: _____

Check out the path below or go online to choose one of the other paths shown.

Investigate Permanent Magnets

- **Hands-On Labs** ✋
- **Magnets in Everyday Life**
- **Propose Your Own Path**

Go online to choose one of these other paths.

Lodestone, like the one in the photo were used for centuries to make compasses. Lodestones are naturally occurring permanent magnets made of iron oxide. This material contains a large amount of iron, as well as the element oxygen. Iron oxide is also called magnetite because of its magnetic properties.

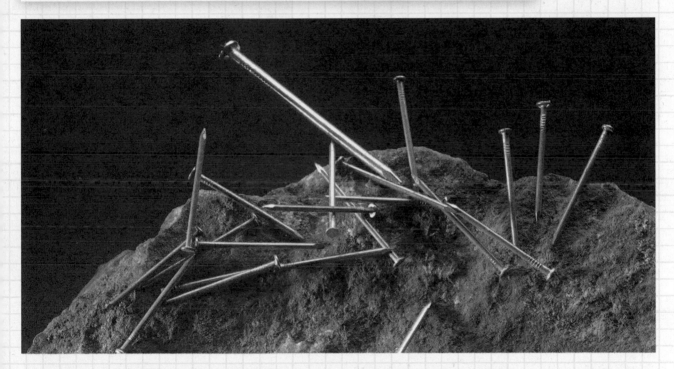

1. A small group of atoms of magnetite will exert less magnetic force than the same number of iron atoms. Despite this, lodestones are permanent magnets, and pure iron is not. How can magnetic domains explain why the magnetic properties of lodestones differ from the properties of pure iron?

   A. The magnetic domains in lodestones are bigger than those in iron.

   B. The poles within each magnetic domain in lodestones line up, but they cancel each other out within each domain in iron.

   C. The magnetic domains in lodestones cannot change their alignment, but those in iron are free to change their orientation.

Continue Your Exploration

The magnet on the left is a ferrite magnet.

200g

1000g

The magnet on the right is a neodymium magnet. The neodymium magnet is much stronger than the ferrite magnet.

Human-Made Magnets

Scientists and engineers have learned how to make magnetic materials. Ferrite is a magnetic material that is composed of iron and oxygen as well as other elements. Rare earth elements, such as neodymium, are also used to make permanent magnets. The magnets made using these rare earth elements are extremely strong.

2. Why might rare earth magnets be so strong? Cite specific details from the lesson about the strength of magnets and magnetic domains to support your answer.

3. How will the effect of a rare earth magnet on a piece of iron compare to the effect of a lodestone on the same piece of iron?

A. Both magnets will be able to move the iron from the same distance.

B. The lodestone will be able to move the iron from a greater distance.

C. The rare earth magnet will be able to move the iron from a greater distance.

D. The lodestone will repel iron, and the rare earth magnet will attract it.

4. Collaborate Compare your answers in this activity with those of a partner. Discuss how you arrived at each answer. Consider how stronger human-made magnets could be created. What would have to be true about a new material in order for it to generate a stronger magnetic force than current magnets do?

Can You Explain It?

Name: _____   Date: _____

> **Why do these rings seem to float without touching one another instead of falling?**

Explore ONLINE!

 EVIDENCE NOTEBOOK

Refer to the notes in your Evidence Notebook to help you construct an explanation for why the rings in the photo levitate instead of simply falling.

1. State your claim. Make sure your claim fully explains how the rings float.

2. Summarize the evidence you have gathered to support your claim and explain your reasoning.

Checkpoints

Answer the following questions to check your understanding of the lesson.

Use the photo to answer Questions 3 and 4.

3. If the magnet on the right is flipped so that the south pole is on the left, the magnetic force will be attractive / repulsive. As the two magnets are moved closer together, the magnetic force between them will become stronger / weaker.

4. If the two magnets were cut in half along the line between the red and blue paint, which statement would describe the four bars that are produced?

   A. Each piece would have one magnetic pole and a nonmagnetic end.

   B. Each piece would have a north pole and a south pole.

   C. Two pieces would only have south poles and the other two pieces would only have north poles.

Use the photo to answer Questions 5 and 6.

5. Which statements describe the iron-containing rock and the nails? Choose all statements that apply.

   A. The rock is a magnet.

   B. The nails are attracted to magnets.

   C. Most of the magnetic domains in the rock are randomly oriented.

   D. Most of the magnetic domains in the rock are aligned with each other.

6. Complete each statement to describe how it would affect the magnetic force present in the photograph.

   A. Removing half of the rock would

   _____ the magnetic force.

   B. Moving the rock and nails higher would

   _____ the magnetic force.

   C. Increasing the distance between the rock and the nails would

   _____ the magnetic force.

   D. Using copper nails instead of iron nails would

   _____ the magnetic force.

   E. Replacing the rock with a similarly sized stronger magnet would

   _____ the magnetic force.

WORD BANK
- increase
- decrease
- not affect

Interactive Review

Complete this section to review the main concepts of the lesson.

A magnet is a material that attracts iron. The force that a magnet generates depends on the strength of the magnet, the distance in between magnetic objects, and the orientation of those objects.

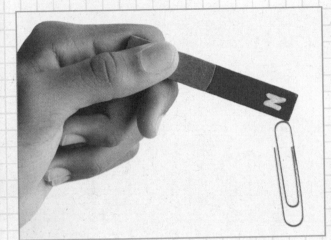

A. A magnet is passed ten centimeters above a desk. A paper clip resting on the desk begins to move as the magnet passes over it. What could be done to increase the effect of the magnet on the paper clip?

The magnetic properties of materials are a result of their atoms and the magnetic domains that form within the material.

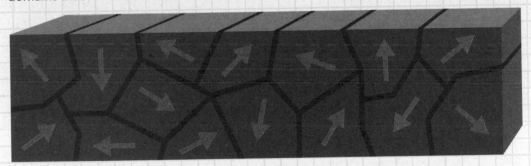

B. The element cobalt displays many similarities to the element iron and is also attracted to magnets. Based on this information, is it likely that cobalt forms magnetic domains? Explain your answer.

Electric Forces

Electricity takes many forms. An electric arc and a lamp lighting up when it is plugged in are both caused by the same basic property of matter.

By the end of this lesson . . .

you will be able to explain how electric charge causes a force and what factors affect the strength of that force.

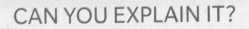Go online to view the digital version of the Hands-On Lab for this lesson and to download additional lab resources.

CAN YOU EXPLAIN IT?

What causes the water droplets to change direction and spiral toward the charged needle?

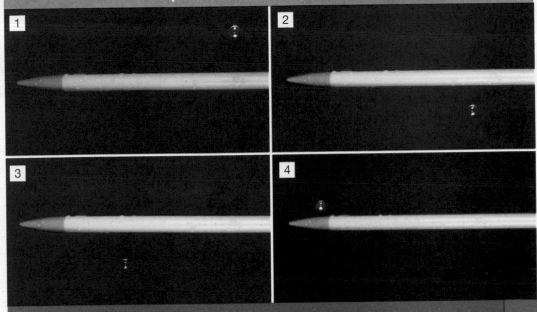

On the International Space Station (ISS), water droplets spiral around this charged knitting needle. Without Earth's gravity pulling objects down, other forces can be observed. Water droplets, like any object, do not change motion unless something pushes or pulls on them.

 **Explore ONLINE!**

1. Why might these water droplets move around the charged knitting needle and change direction?

2. What are some other examples of a force acting on an object without touching it?

 EVIDENCE NOTEBOOK As you explore the lesson, gather evidence to help explain the behavior of the water droplets on the ISS.

Analyzing Electric Charge

You might feel a shock when you touch a metal object, such as a doorknob, especially when the weather is dry. If it is dark enough, you may even see a spark. This spark is caused by a property of matter.

3. **Write** Use the space below or write on a piece of paper. What do you think causes these sparks to form? Write about a time that you saw sparks, and try to identify the conditions that caused the sparks.

Electric Charge

Electric charge is a physical property of all matter. Every type of electricity is the result of electric charge. Electric charges moving through wires are used to run many everyday devices, such as lamps and computers. Static electricity, which can cause your hair to stick up, is caused by electric charges that are not moving. Moving charges can cause sparks. When you touch a doorknob and are shocked, electric charges that had been on your hand or on the doorknob quickly move between objects, causing a spark.

Electric charges in fabric can cause clothing to stick together. Electrical devices also use electric charge. Electrical devices work because electric charges can move through wires.

Signs of Electric Charges

Electric charges can be positive or negative. Positive charges are represented by a plus sign (+), and negative charges are represented by a negative sign (−). The sign of a charge affects how it interacts with other charges. Objects tend to have many positive and negative charges. Most objects are neutral, meaning they have no net charge. Think about what happens when you add −1 and 1. The result is zero ($-1 + 1 = 0$). Adding positive and negative charges is the same as adding positive and negative numbers. An object with an equal number of positive and negative charges has a net charge of zero. A positively charged object has more positive charges than negative charges. A negatively charged object has more negative charges than positive charges.

4. Static electricity is caused by an imbalance of electric charge. When positive charges build up on an object, the object has a net positive charge. When negative charges build up on an object, the object has a net *positive / negative / neutral* charge. An electric discharge happens when an object loses its extra charge. The positive and negative charges in an object are equal after a complete discharge, so the object has a net *positive / negative / neutral* charge.

The Conservation of Charge

The net charge on an object can change. A neutral object can become positively or negatively charged. The amount of net charge on an object can increase or decrease, and charged objects can even become neutral. When the amount of net charge on an object changes, electric charges are never created or destroyed. Instead, charges have been transferred between objects.

Forces are needed to separate positive and negative charges because opposite charges are attracted to each other. If possible, opposite charges tend to move toward one another, which leads to many objects having a net neutral charge. Outside forces or energy can be used to separate opposite charges. For instance, friction between two materials can increase the rate at which charges separate. When you drag your feet across the carpet, the carpet can transfer negative charges to you. You become negatively charged, and the carpet becomes positively charged.

When a balloon is rubbed against a person's hair, negative electric charges move from the hair to the balloon. The total number of positive and negative charges does not change when charges move between objects.

5. How is the person in the photos separating the charges in her hair and the balloon?

6. What do you notice about the net charges of the balloon and the hair after electric charges moved between them?

Both the balloon and the person's hair are charged. The balloon is negatively charged because it has more negative charges than positive charges. The hair is positively charged because it has more positive charges than negative charges.

7. Engineer It Preventing charge from building up is necessary on some job sites. The buildup of charge may be a safety hazard or could damage products. A company wants to design a device to minimize the buildup of charge on an object. Which of the following materials would be the best choice to make such a device out of?

A. aluminum, which transfers charge quickly

B. rubber, which barely transfers charge

C. a new plastic, which transfers charge at a moderate pace

Charges in Neutral Objects

Generally, positive and negative charges are evenly spread out in an object. Opposite charges are attracted to one another and similar charges are repelled from one another. This leads to charges spreading out evenly throughout an object. However, charges can move in a neutral object. Wires generally have a neutral charge, but electric charges can move freely through them. Charges are also able to move and separate within an object if exposed to outside forces.

Opposite charges pull on each other, while similar charges push on each other. This balloon has a negative charge. The balloon is attracted to the wall, even though the wall has an overall neutral charge.

8. Discuss The wall did not seem to have a charge until the negatively charged balloon was put near it. With a partner, consider the options and determine how the wall could have become charged.

A. The wall transferred electric charges to the balloon.

B. The balloon transferred electric charges to the wall.

C. Positive charges in the wall moved to align with the balloon's negative charges.

D. The wall gained positive charges to balance the balloon's extra negative charges.

Movement of Charge within Neutral Objects

A charged object can make the charges in a neutral object move. For example, a negatively charged object pulls positive charges toward it and pushes negative charges away from it. As a result, parts of the neutral object become negatively charged, and other parts become positively charged. When the charged object is moved away, the positive charges and negative charges in the neutral object move and become evenly spread out again.

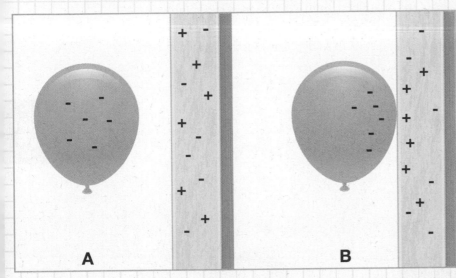

A

B

Placing a negatively charged balloon near a neutral wall causes the negative charges in the wall to move away from the balloon. The now positively charged surface of the wall and the negatively charged balloon are attracted to each other.

EVIDENCE NOTEBOOK

9. Water droplets tend to have a neutral charge. How might they still be affected by the charges of other objects? Record your evidence.

Analyze Charge in a Cloud

All matter, even clouds, has the property of electric charge. A charge imbalance causes static electricity within the cloud. At times, the charges on a pair of clouds or on a cloud and the ground neutralize by discharging. The discharge appears as lightning.

10. During thunderstorms, positive and negative charges in clouds become separated. Positive charge builds up on the top of clouds, and negative charge builds up on the bottom of clouds. How might the charged clouds affect the charges in the neutral ground below the clouds? Describe what happens to the charges in the ground.

_____

_____

_____

_____

_____

_____

Measuring the Electric Force

The Electric Force

The **electric force** is the force of attraction or repulsion between objects due to their charges. The electric force can push or pull on objects from a distance. It is similar to gravity in that it can act on objects without touching them. The electric force can cause a charged balloon to stick to a wall or a sock to stick to a shirt. The electric force can also be used to make a plastic film float in midair.

Explore ONLINE!

The plastic film would usually fall to the ground, but the balloon keeps it floating in the air. The balloon and the plastic film are both negatively charged.

11. The plastic film and the balloon are able to affect each other's motion because they are charged. What does this tell you about how electric charge causes the objects to interact with each other?

EVIDENCE NOTEBOOK

12. Do you think that the water droplets that spiral around the charged needle on the ISS might experience an electric force? Record your evidence.

Hands-On Lab
Explore the Electric Force

Part 1: Variables that Affect the Electric Force

You will develop and answer questions to determine the variables that affect the strength and direction of electric force. What affects how fast a ball moves? When you throw a ball, you are applying a force. How quickly you move your arm is a variable that affects the force's strength. Variables also affect the strength of an electric force.

MATERIALS
- balloons, inflated to about the same size (2)
- measuring tape
- paper towels
- piece of wool
- thread or fishing line

Procedure and Analysis

STEP 1 Rub the balloons on your hair or on the wool. This gives the balloons a negative charge and your hair or the wool a positive charge. The more you rub the balloons against your hair or the wool, the greater the magnitude of the negative charge on the balloons.

STEP 2 Experiment to see how the charged objects affect one another. Answer the guiding questions below, and develop at least two additional questions to answer. To remove the net charge from a balloon, wipe it with a damp paper towel and then dry it.

Guiding Questions

- How do the balloons affect each other's motion?
- How do the balloons affect the motion of hair or wool?

STEP 3 On a separate sheet of paper, record your procedure and observations in a table like the one shown below.

Guiding Question	My Procedure	Observations

STEP 4 **Discuss** Together with a partner, look over the data you gathered. Compare your observations and determine which factors seem to affect the strength of the electric force. Choose all that apply.

A. distance between objects

B. magnitude of the charges

C. mass of objects

D. sign of the charges

Sign of the Electric Charge

You observed that the electric force can push balloons with similar charges away from each other. The electric force also pulls oppositely charged objects, such as your hair and the balloon, together. The sign of the electric charges determines whether the electric force pushes or pulls on objects. When objects have like charges, they repel each other. When objects have opposite charges, they attract each other.

The diagram shows how the electric force affects the motion of positive and negative charges. Notice that positive charges repel each other, negative charges repel each other, and positive and negative charges attract each other. The sign of the electric charge does not affect the strength of the electric force. An object with a charge of $+1$ generates the same strength of electric force as an object with a charge of -1. Neutral objects, which have a charge of zero, do not typically exert an electric force.

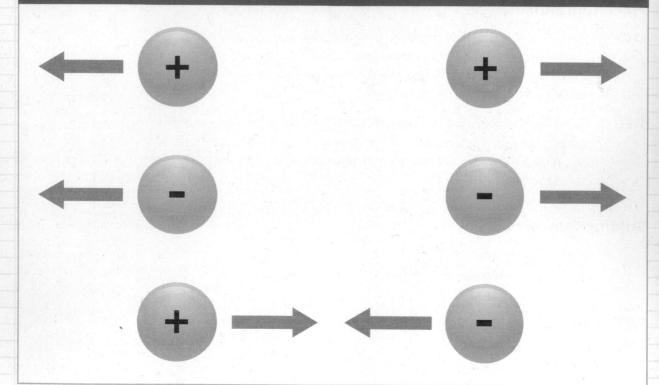

Charge Sign and Force Direction

13. Recharge your balloons and hold them gently by their knots. Move the balloons near one another. What does your observation tell you about the electric charges of the balloons?

Part 2: Distance between Charged Objects

In Part 1, you determined that distance is a factor that affects the strength of the electric force. You will formulate a hypothesis to test how distance between two charged balloons affects the electric force. You will then use your observations as evidence to construct a claim.

Procedure and Analysis

STEP 1 Work with a partner to develop a question to guide your exploration.

STEP 2 Based on your question and previous observations, frame a hypothesis. Be sure to include the independent and dependent variables.

STEP 3 Use the two balloons from the previous activity. Tie a thread around the knot of one balloon. Hang the balloon from a desk, a lab stand, or the ceiling.

STEP 4 Rub both balloons against your hair or the piece of wool ten times to charge them. Be sure to charge all around the balloons, not just one spot.

STEP 5 Let the balloon tied to the thread hang freely. Move the other balloon close to the hanging balloon. Observe what happens. Experiment with how the distance between the balloons affects the electric force

STEP 6 **Language SmArts** Construct a claim of how distance between charged objects affects the electric force. Support your claim using evidence from your observations.

EVIDENCE NOTEBOOK

14. How might the distance between the needle and the water droplets have affected the movement of the droplets? Record your evidence.

The hanging balloons will separate when the force between them increases. If the force decreases, the balloons will fall so that they hang straight down.

Part 3: Magnitude of the Electric Charge

How does the number of charges on objects affect the force between them? You will investigate how the magnitude of electric charge on an object affects the electric force. You will record your data in the table on the next page. As you complete the investigation, consider how you will answer the guiding question.

Both positive and negative electric charges can have different magnitudes. For example, the electric charge on an object with three positive charges on it has a greater magnitude than the electric charge on an object with one positive charge on it. The magnitude of the charge depends on how many extra positive or negative charges build up on the object. The sign of the net charge on an object does not change the magnitude of the charge. For example, a positive charge of +2 and a negative charge of –2 both have a magnitude of 2.

Guiding Question

What effect does increasing the charge on the balloons have on the electric force?

Procedure and Analysis

STEP 1 Place two desks about 50 cm apart. Tie two pieces of thread to the knot of each balloon. Hang the first balloon between the desks by taping the loose end of one thread to the edge of one desk and taping the loose end of the other piece of thread to the edge of the other desk. The balloon should hang loosely between the desks. Hang the second balloon by taping the threads to the same spots as for the first balloon. The two balloons should be touching when they hang freely.

STEP 2 Rub each balloon on your hair/wool once. Make sure to rub each side of the balloons to charge them evenly. Let both balloons hang freely. Record your observations and measure the distance between the two balloons.

STEP 3 Rub each balloon two more times, and repeat your measurements from Step 2.

STEP 4 Repeat Step 3, this time choosing the number of times to rub each balloon between measurements. Repeat this step, giving you four total distances.

STEP 5 Develop two additional questions to explore using these materials. Using the balloons, try to answer these questions and expand your understanding.

Total number of rubs on each balloon	Distance between balloons

STEP 6 **Do the Math** You can use graphs to identify the relationship between variables. Make a graph of your data to see how the total number of rubs affects the distance between the two balloons.

STEP 7 Look at the relationship between the total number of times you rubbed the balloon and the distance as shown on your graph. What can you determine about how the magnitude of the electric charge affects the electric force between charged objects?

15. Compare the two pairs of charged objects. Which pair of objects, A or B, has a stronger electric force between the two objects? Explain your answer.

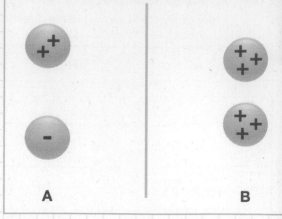

A   B

The diagram shows two pairs of charged objects. The number of signs in each object represents the magnitude of the charge.

Analyze the Force on a Stream of Water

Electric force pushes and pulls on objects without touching them. The electric force between objects with like charges pushes the objects apart. The electric force between objects with opposite charges pulls the objects together. The electric force increases as the magnitude of the charge increases and as the distance between objects decreases. Think about what you know about electric charge and electric force.

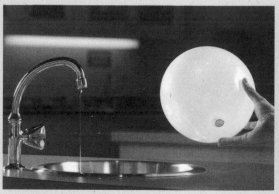

The balloon has a negative charge and water is neutral. They are far enough apart so that the electric force is very weak.

16. Water molecules are neutral. Even though the electric charges are balanced in each molecule, one side of the molecule is slightly positive and the other side is slightly negative. Why does the stream of water bend toward the negatively charged balloon in the bottom photo?

_____

_____

_____

_____

_____

_____

Moving the charged balloon toward the water causes the stream of water to bend. The water is attracted to the balloon, but it is still pulled down by gravity.

EVIDENCE NOTEBOOK

17. Could the water droplets in the ISS pictures be affected in the same way as this stream of water is being affected? Record your evidence.

Continue Your Exploration

Name: _____   Date: _____

Check out the path below or go online to choose one of the other paths shown.

Static Electricity

- **Experimenting with the Charges of Materials**
- **Propose Your Own Path**

Go online to choose one of these other paths.

Van de Graaff generators are used to demonstrate static electricity. Static electricity is the buildup of charge. Negative charge builds up when an object gains more negative charges than positive charges. Positive charge builds up when an object gains more positive charges than negative charges. These extra charges are eventually transferred to other objects.

A Van de Graaff generator can be used to explore static electricity. A large number of positive charges build up on the sphere of a Van de Graaff generator.

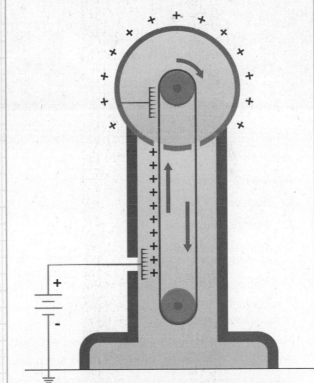

When the Van de Graaff generator is turned on, a belt moves. The Van de Graaff generator removes negative electric charges from the moving belt, giving the belt a positive charge. Negative charges from the sphere are then attracted to the belt, leaving the sphere with a positive charge.

Continue Your Exploration

A student touches a highly charged Van de Graaff generator. Charge moves between the student and the generator, causing the student to become charged.

1. What causes your hair to stand up when you touch the sphere of a Van de Graaff generator?

   A. gravity

   B. buoyancy

   C. electric discharge

   D. static electricity

2. The sphere of the Van de Graaff generator builds up positive charge on its surface. If you touch the sphere, you will gain *positive / negative / no* charges.

3. Your hair strands have *positive / negative / no* charges on them when you are touching the generator. Since your hair strands are
   attracted / repelled by one another due to the electric force, they are *similarly / oppositely* charged.

4. **Collaborate** Together with a partner, discuss your understanding of Van de Graaff generators. Make a model that shows how the charges in objects would behave if the objects touched a Van de Graaff generator.

Can You Explain It?

Name: <u>   </u>   **Date:** <u>   </u>

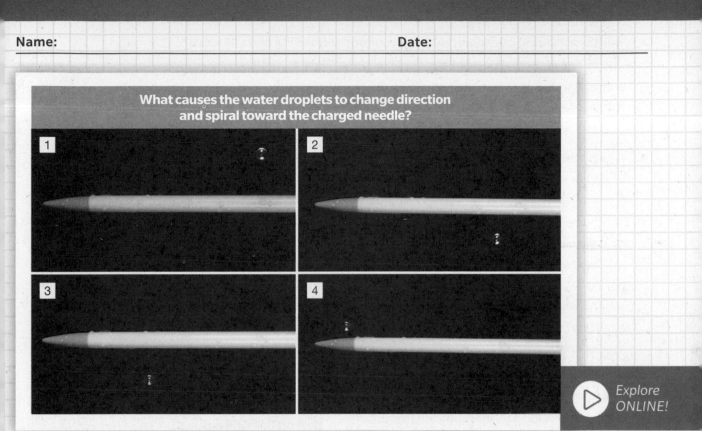

What causes the water droplets to change direction and spiral toward the charged needle?

EVIDENCE NOTEBOOK

Refer to the notes in your Evidence Notebook to help you construct an explanation for why the water drops seem to orbit the charged needle.

1. State your claim. Make sure your claim fully explains why the water droplets change direction and spiral toward the charged needle.

2. Summarize the evidence you have gathered to support your claim and explain your reasoning.

Checkpoints

Answer the following questions to check your understanding of the lesson.

Use the image of the balloons to answer Questions 3 and 4.

3. Both balloons are ~~negatively~~ / positively charged.
   A force pushes the balloons away from each other because they are
   ~~oppositely~~ / similarly charged.

4. Which statements describe how the electric force affects the balloons? Choose all that apply.

   A. The balloons are pulled together by the electric force.

   B. The balloons are pushed apart by the electric force.

   C. The balloons stick together once they are touching because they need to be in contact to be affected by the electric force.

   D. If the balloons move closer together, the electric force acting on them increases.

   E. If one of the balloons becomes positively charged, the electric force increases.

Use the image of the comb to answer Questions 5 and 6.

5. A student conducts an investigation to find out whether the electric force of a charged object—a comb—is strong enough to pick up a very light, neutral object—foam packing peanuts. To charge the comb, the student rubs the comb with a wool cloth. The cloth becomes positively charged. The student then holds the comb above the foam packing peanuts. The results are shown in the photo. Choose the symbol that represents the charge on the comb and on a packing peanut:

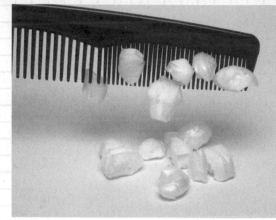

   A. Charge of the comb: + / − / 0

   B. Charge of the side of a packing peanut that is not touching the comb: + / − / 0

   C. Charge of the side of a packing peanut that is touching the comb: + / − / 0

6. The packing peanuts are removed from the comb and placed on the table. Then the positively charged wool cloth is held close to the packing peanuts. What will happen to the packing peanuts?

   A. They will stick to the wool cloth.

   B. They will be pushed away from the wool cloth.

   C. They will not be affected by the wool cloth.

Interactive Review

Complete this section to review the main concepts of the lesson.

Electric charge is a physical property of all matter. Electric charge can be positive or negative and objects can have overall negative, positive, or neutral charges.

A. When clothes are run through a dryer they often become charged and stick together. What causes the charges to separate?

Charged objects generate an electric force between them. The direction of the force is determined by the signs of the charges. The strength depends on the magnitude and the distance.

B. Two particles are moving toward one another. Both of the particles have a strong positive charge. As they move toward one another, how will the electric force between the two particles change?

Fields

This amazing display of swirling colors is called an aurora. The colored lights are the result of charged particles from solar winds interacting with Earth's magnetic field.

By the end of this lesson . . .

you will be able to describe and model the effects of electric, magnetic, and gravitational fields on objects within these fields.

Go *online* to view the digital version of the Hands-On Lab for this lesson and to download additional lab resources.

CAN YOU EXPLAIN IT?

Is a stink field a real field?

These people are reacting to something unpleasant. Which of their senses is being affected? Do you think it is something they can see or touch? Whatever it is, it must be able to travel through air. What do you think it might be? What could the people do to stop the unpleasant experience?

Yuck! These people are reacting to a stinky odor from garbage. Plugging your nose might help block the smell for a while, but you cannot hold your nose forever. Would you be surprised to learn that the smell of stinky garbage is similar to the way electrical, gravitational, and magnetic forces affect objects? An analogy is a way to learn about a concept by comparing it to a concept that you already know. To understand the analogy, let's start by thinking about what affects the bad smell from garbage.

1. On a hot day, the garbage stink covers a *larger / smaller* area than on a cool day.

2. I would rather sit near the garbage can when it is full of *boiled cabbage / stale bread.*

3. The smell from the garbage can is *stronger / weaker* when I sit farther from the garbage.

4. Adding more garbage to the can makes the smell *stronger / weaker.*

5. People passing the garbage can are usually *affected / not affected* by the smell coming from the garbage can.

EVIDENCE NOTEBOOK As you explore the lesson, gather evidence to help explain whether a stink field is a good analogy for other types of fields.

Evaluating Evidence of Fields

When you throw a ball into the air, you must touch it to apply the force that makes the ball move upward. Yet gravity pulls the ball back toward Earth even though the ball is not touching the ground. You can use a magnet to hold a picture to a metal locker. The magnet does not need to touch the locker to hold the picture in place. Gravity and magnetism, two forces that can act at a distance without touching an object, are examples of noncontact forces.

Noncontact forces only affect objects within a certain area. Think about a spider sitting on its web. Prey that lands will exert a force on the web. The spider will detect that force from anywhere on its web. Similarly, any magnetic object that enters the area around the locker will experience a force, and the locker will also experience that force. Like the odor from garbage, you cannot see magnetic forces, but they can have an effect on you or other objects.

6. **Draw** Think about your experiences with magnets. Draw and describe what happens if you slowly move a magnet toward a pile of iron paper clips.

The force applied by prey landing on a spider's web sends vibrations outward through the strands of the web.

If the spider is on the web, it feels the vibrations and moves quickly to pounce on the prey.

▶ *Explore ONLINE!*

Fields in Science

What do you think of when you hear the word *field*? Maybe you imagine a large grassy meadow with wildflowers, a baseball diamond, or a profession, such as teaching. These meanings are all correct, but they are not what *field* means in science. In science, a **field** is the area in which an object experiences a force that acts at a distance.

Fields can be tricky to study because they do not have mass. However, scientists know fields exist because they can detect the force or energy in the field. The force or energy cannot be detected outside of the field. One way that scientists can study fields is by creating a model, or a series of models, of the field.

The force arrows show that while both the leaf and the dog are being pulled toward Earth by gravity, the gravitational force acting on the leaf is smaller than the gravitational force acting on the dog.

The uniformly spaced field lines show that the gravitational field is uniform at the surface of Earth. Everything on the surface of Earth, including the leaf and the dog, are inside Earth's gravitational field.

Forces and Fields

You probably remember that a force is a push or a pull exerted on an object. All forces have size and direction and can change the acceleration of an object. Arrows can be used to model the forces acting on an object. You know that the falling motion of the leaf in the picture is evidence that a gravitational force is pulling the leaf toward Earth. Of course, just because a force is acting on an object does not mean that you will see motion. For example, gravitational force is also acting on the dog, even though the dog is not moving.

Gravitational forces act on the leaf, the dog, and everything else inside of Earth's gravitational field—even the air around you! Like scientists, you can learn about a field by analyzing models of fields. One type of field model is made up of arrows called *field lines*. First, the field is measured. Then, the data can be mapped using field lines. The direction of the field lines models the direction of the forces acting in that field. The spacing between field lines indicates the strength of the field. The closer the field lines are to one another, the stronger the field is. The equally spaced field lines in the image above show that the strength of the field is the same for all objects in the field.

EVIDENCE NOTEBOOK

7. Look at the pictures of people smelling stinky garbage at the beginning of the lesson. Use what you have learned about fields and field lines to describe each person's reaction to the garbage they have encountered.

Gravitational Fields

Because every object has mass, every object exerts a gravitational force and has a gravitational field around it. The **gravitational field** is the area surrounding an object in which another object is pulled toward the object. The gravitational field of the sun includes the entire solar system because all objects in the solar system are pulled toward the sun. Gravitational field lines point toward the object that is exerting the force. For example, the sun's gravitational field is represented by lines that point toward the center of the sun. You learned that the density of the field lines represents the strength of gravitational fields. Notice that the sun's gravitational field is strongest at the surface of the sun. The strength of the field decreases as the distance from the sun increases until the field can no longer be detected.

The sun's large gravitational field keeps Earth and every other object in the solar system in orbit around it.

The pattern of field lines can also show how two fields interact. For example, the pattern of field lines around Earth and the moon identify areas where the attractive forces increase the strength of the field and where they cancel each other out. As the moon orbits Earth, the field around the moon moves with it. By studying the field lines in a series of models, a scientist could analyze how the fields change over time.

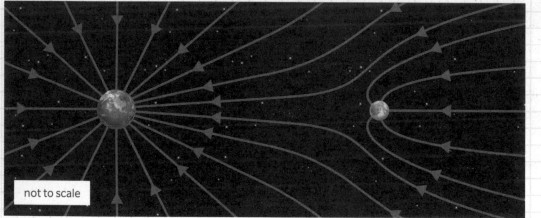

not to scale

The lines around Earth are closer together than the lines around the moon. This means that Earth's gravitational field is stronger than the moon's. Earth's stronger gravitational field keeps the moon in orbit.

8. Compare the patterns of field lines in each gravitational field model. What can you conclude about the strength of the fields from the models? Choose all statements that apply.

   A. The strength of the gravitational field is the same at the surface of the sun, Earth, and the moon.

   B. The strength of the sun's gravitational field decreases as the distance from the sun increases.

   C. The moon's gravitational field does not affect Earth.

   D. The gravitational field at Earth's surface is greater than the gravitational field at the moon's surface.

Electric Fields

Most objects have an equal number of positive and negative charges, so most objects are neutral. However, some objects have more positive charges than negative charges, and the object is said to be positively charged. Other objects have more negative charges, so they are negatively charged. Every charged object is surrounded by an electric field. An **electric field** is the area around a charged object in which another charged object is affected by the electric force. The strength and size of an electric field depends on the magnitude of the electric charge. The bigger the charge, the stronger and larger its electric field. As with gravitational fields, the electric field decreases as the distance from the charged object increases.

The electric field around a charged object pulls oppositely charged objects toward the charged object and pushes similarly charged objects away. For example, when you rub your foot on a carpet, the carpet will give up negative charges to become positively charged, while your body gains negative charges to become negatively charged. When you touch another object that has a positive charge, the electric fields of your body and the object pull the opposite charges toward each other. The negative charges can suddenly flow to the other object, resulting in an electric discharge. When this sudden flow happens, you feel a shock.

9. Imagine that a sock is stuck to the jeans you just pulled out of the dryer. Do the two items have the same or opposite charge? Explain your answer.

Explore ONLINE!

Experiment with Charged Objects in an Electric Field

The student wipes a plastic rod with a wool cloth and then suspends it. When the negatively charged wool cloth enters the positively charged rod's field, the oppositely charged objects are attracted to each other.

The student wipes a second plastic rod with the wool cloth. She then moves the positively charged rod toward the suspended rod. The two positively charged rods repel each other.

Model Electric Fields

Wool fibers are mixed into oil in the image below. An electric charge from the metal plates is applied to the mixture. When a charge is applied, the fibers line up to reveal the pattern of the electric field. The pattern depends on whether the charges are the same or opposite.

10. Analyze the pattern of the field lines in this model. Do they show that the plates are attracting or repelling each other? Fill in the missing charge to make the model correct.

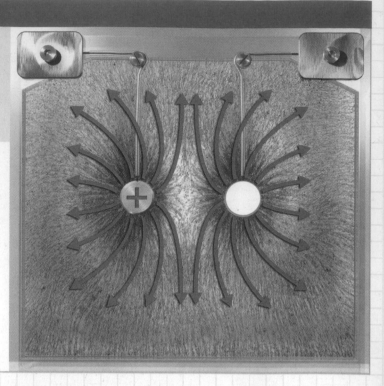

11. Does the model above show a pushing or a pulling force? Explain your answer.

To model electric fields consistently, field lines always point away from positive charges and toward negative charges. When two charged objects are near each other, the pattern of the field lines shows the overall strength of each field at different locations. For example, when the fields of two opposite or like charges interact, the resulting field between the objects is strong. When two like charges interact, the field lines show that charges push away from each other. And when opposite charges interact, the field lines show that the charges are attracted to each other.

Magnetic Fields

Every magnet is surrounded by a **magnetic field**—the area around a magnet in which magnetic forces affect magnetic objects. You can feel the magnetic field when you hold two magnets near each other. If you put both north poles or both south poles near each other, they will push apart. But if you put a north pole and a south pole near each other, the magnets will pull together.

The strength of a magnetic field depends on the strength of the magnet. The field is strongest near each pole of the magnet and decreases as the distance from the pole increases. Field lines represent these characteristics of magnetic fields. They are closest together near the poles where the magnetic field is the strongest. The arrows of magnetic field lines point away from the north pole and toward the south pole.

12. The density of the iron filings shows the strength of the magnetic field. Rank the strength of the magnetic field in different spots by labeling where the field is strong, medium, and weak.

Analyze Magnetic Fields

Tiny pieces of iron are pulled toward the magnet by the magnetic field. The iron filings line up to reveal the pattern of the magnetic field. If you wanted to create a model of the field using field lines, the arrows would point away from the north pole and toward the south pole.

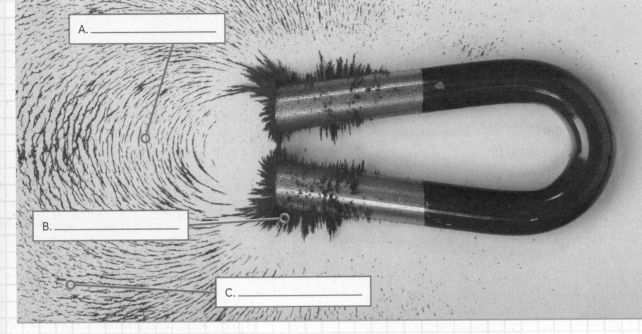

A. _____

B. _____

C. _____

13. Do the Math One common characteristic of fields is that they are all stronger at close distances. The farther away an object is from the source of the field, the less affected the object is by the field. Look at table to see how the force due to a magnetic field changes with distance. In the third column, record the change in force between the measurement in that row and the previous measurement. The first two rows have been done for you.

Distance from Magnet (m)	Strength of Magnetic Force (N)	Change in Force (N)
1.00	100	n/a
2.00	25	-75
3.00	11.1	
4.00	6.25	
5.00	4	

14. Circle the true statements based on your knowledge of fields.

A. Fields decrease in strength as distance increases.

B. The rate of change in a field's strength with distance is constant. Each increase in distance has the same effect on the strength of the field.

Analyze Evidence for Fields

Scientists developed the idea of fields to explain how gravity, electric force, and magnetic force can affect objects without touching them. The idea of fields is accepted today because scientists have gathered and carefully analyzed a vast amount of evidence for each of the three forces.

Scientists find evidence for gravitational fields as they analyze information about how gravity affects the organization and motion of objects throughout the universe. They have analyzed information about electric fields to explain why all charged objects need to be a certain distance from each other before they are attracted or repelled. Data collected and analyzed about the predictable behavior of magnets provides evidence of magnetic fields.

15. The table below shows evidence for this claim: **Objects are affected by the fields of noncontact forces**. Analyze the evidence and complete the table by filling in the Supports Claim and Reasoning columns. Use the example in the first column to guide your answers.

Evidence	Supports Claim (Yes / No)	Reasoning
Maglev trains hover above the track.	Yes	The magnets in the train and the track exert pushing forces on each other.
If you rub your hair with a balloon, the balloon and your hair attract each other when they are close. They do not attract each other when they are far apart.		
A bike slows down if you do not pedal as its wheels roll over pavement.		
The moons of Jupiter orbit Jupiter because they are pulled toward Jupiter. The moons of Jupiter are too far to be pulled into Earth's orbit.		

16. **Discuss** Together with a partner, compare your tables. What can you conclude based on the evidence in the table? What scientific questions do you still have about fields that you could test in different ways? Record two questions about fields and how they could be tested.

EVIDENCE NOTEBOOK

17. Think about what affects the strength of a field. Compare the stinky garbage at the beginning of the lesson to magnetic, electric, and gravitational fields. Identify the factors that affect the strength of each field. Are there similar factors that affect the strength of the garbage's stink? Record your evidence.

Investigate Earth's Electric Field

In addition to having a gravitational field, Earth also has an electric field. The electric field is the result of positive charges in the upper atmosphere and negative charges at Earth's surface. The field is stronger at higher altitudes and weaker near Earth's surface, which is why you usually do not notice it. However, you do notice electric fields in the atmosphere during thunderstorms. During a thunderstorm, the electric field is reversed, with excess negative charges at the bottom of storm clouds and excess positive charges at the ground. You can see the lightning that results from the electric field.

18. **Draw** Look at the model and think about what you learned about electric field lines. Draw arrows to complete the model of Earth's electric field on a sunny day.

Modeling Fields

Scientists Are Still Learning about Fields

Scientists understand a lot about fields, but they are still making new discoveries about them all the time. For example, studies of distant black holes in space have led to new understanding of gravitational fields. Black holes cannot be seen. Scientists detect them by working together to gather and analyze data about how black holes pull in nearby matter. From their analysis, scientists have learned that the gravitational field of a black hole is so strong that the space around it curves so that even light cannot escape.

Recently, scientists who develop mathematical computer models of black holes have made an even more surprising discovery. The data they have recently analyzed shows that the gravitational fields of black holes may make the space around them bumpy, like choppy water.

This artist's conception depicts how the strong gravity of a black hole is affecting the gas, matter, and light around it. Because we can't see black holes, scientists use special tools to find and study them.

19. **Write** Use the space below or write on a sheet of paper. How does the discovery that gravitational fields may make the space around them bumpy show that collaborating and investigating new ideas are important in science?

Model Magnetic Fields

What patterns can you discover in magnetic fields? You have seen the pattern iron filings make around a horseshoe magnet. Now you will investigate the fields around bar magnets in different combinations and orientations and create models of the resulting fields.

MATERIALS
- iron filings, in a sealed bag
- magnets, assorted
- paper

Iron filings line up along the magnetic field. Scientists use observations like this one to make models of magnetic fields.

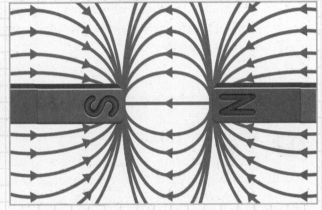

Field lines are used to model the strength, size, and direction of the magnetic field around one or more magnets.

Procedure

STEP 1 On a separate sheet of paper, plan an investigation using the materials provided to model the magnetic fields around magnets. Use field lines to make models for at least three different combinations of magnets. Think about the steps you will follow in your investigation. Check off the questions you considered.

Questions to Consider:	✓
What question about magnetic fields around magnets do you want to answer?	
Which combinations of magnets are you going to use? How will you orient the poles of the magnets?	
How will you observe the magnetic fields around the magnets?	
What information should you show in your model to represent the magnetic field?	
What have you learned about magnetic field lines that you should include in your model?	

Analysis

STEP 2 Record your procedure steps and observations in a table like the one shown.

Question I Am Investigating:		
Procedure Step	Observations	Drawing of Model

STEP 3 **Discuss** With a partner, evaluate each other's procedure. Then individually on a separate sheet of paper, write an argument that explains why the model you made provides evidence that magnetic fields exist between magnets that are not touching. Explain why you chose your model and why you considered certain designs.

EVIDENCE NOTEBOOK

20. In your own words, explain what a field is. Use examples from the investigation. Does your explanation apply to the stink around a pile of garbage? Record your evidence.

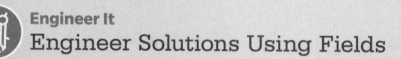

Engineer It
Engineer Solutions Using Fields

Explore ONLINE!

Investigations of fields help astronomers understand how fields work and help engineers develop interesting new materials. Some of these materials may even be used to treat diseases.

Scientists and engineers are investigating how to use ferrofluids to deliver medication directly where it is needed in the body. This procedure could be important for cancer treatments. Doctors use drugs to kill cancer tumors, but these drugs can also kill healthy cells because delivering the treatment to only the cancer cells is not easy to do,

21. When the magnetic field is removed, the ferrofluid becomes liquid / toxic.

22. One potential advantage of using a ferrofluid to deliver medicine is that it can be directed to tumors by a magnetic field / is cheaper than existing treatments.

Ferrofluids are a mixture of tiny magnetic particles and a liquid. Ferrofluids look and act like other liquids, unless they are in a strong magnetic field. When exposed to a magnetic field, the ferrofluid forms spikes that look and act like solids.

Continue Your Exploration

Name: _____ **Date:** _____

Check out the path below or go online to choose one of the other paths shown.

> Earth's Magnetic Field

- **Hands-On Labs** ✋
- **Can Bumblebees See Electric Fields?**
- **Propose Your Own Path**

Go online to choose one of these other paths.

Earth is like a giant bar magnet and is surrounded by a huge magnetic field. Earth's core is an enormous mass of heavy elements, such as iron and nickel. The magnetic field is created when the solid inner core and the flowing molten metals in the liquid part of Earth's outer core interact.

Humans and other animals, such as sea turtles, use Earth's magnetic field to navigate around the globe. As scientists and engineers discover new information about Earth's magnetic field, they can create new ways to use it.

Earth's Poles

The north pole of a compass needle is a magnetic north pole. It is attracted to the geographic North Pole, which is a magnetic south pole. It sounds confusing, but think about it—like all other magnets, Earth has a north pole and a south pole that interact with other magnets. Earth's geographic North Pole attracts the north end of other magnets, so, because opposite poles attract, Earth's geographic North Pole is actually the south pole of Earth's magnetic field. It is called the north magnetic pole because it is in the Northern Hemisphere. It might help to think of Earth's magnetic north pole as the place on Earth that the north pole of magnets point to.

Throughout Earth's history, the north and south magnetic poles have changed places many times. When the poles change places, the direction of Earth's magnetic field changes. This change is called a magnetic reversal. Igneous rock layers contain a record of magnetic reversals. Iron is found in igneous rocks, which form from magma. While the iron is molten, the domains in iron align themselves with Earth's magnetic field like tiny compass needles.

Earth's magnetic field is similar to the magnetic field of a bar magnet that is tilted when compared to Earth's rotational axis.

Continue Your Exploration

1. The current magnetic north pole is near the geographic North Pole, but they are not in exactly the same place. Compasses point toward the north magnetic pole. How does a compass needle help people find the direction that they are going?

2. Most people need a compass to navigate using magnetic fields, but birds, whales, deer, and many other organisms have the ability to detect Earth's magnetic fields without a compass. The mechanism that many organisms use to detect the magnetic field is still not entirely understood. However, the mechanisms of a group of bacteria that align with the magnetic field of Earth are well understood. The bacteria provide scientists with a simple organism that they can study to find out how organisms can naturally detect magnetic fields. What would be a reasonable hypothesis about how these bacteria detect the magnetic field?

   A. The bacteria respond to electric fields.

   B. The bacteria have iron particles in their bodies.

   C. The bacteria can see magnetic fields.

   D. The bacteria can detect gravity.

3. Bacteria that can detect magnetic fields are called *magnetotactic bacteria*. They naturally contain particles, such as magnetite, that are affected by magnetic fields. These particles form short chains in the bacteria that line up along magnetic fields, similar to the way a compass needle aligns with Earth's magnetic field. Scientists can use fossils of these magnetotactic bacteria to study what Earth's magnetic field was like in the past. Rocks that formed from cooling lava can also contain clues about the history of Earth's magnetic field. Which of the following statements is not true?

   A. Rocks that contain iron are affected by Earth's magnetic field.

   B. The magnetic fields of magnetic materials in molten rock align with Earth's magnetic field.

   C. When the poles reverse, the magnetic fields in both fossilized and molten rock reverse.

   D. Rocks contain a record of Earth's changing magnetic field.

4. **Collaborate** Together with a small group, predict possible local and global impacts of a reversal of Earth's magnetic field.

Can You Explain It?

Name: _____   Date: _____

Is a stink field a real field?

EVIDENCE NOTEBOOK

Refer to the notes in your Evidence Notebook to help you construct an explanation for whether the area around stinky garbage is a real field. Comparing two things in order to learn about one is an analogy.

1. State your claim. Make sure your claim fully explains how a stink field compares to electric, magnetic, and gravitational fields.

2. Summarize the evidence you have gathered to support your claim and explain your reasoning.

Checkpoints

Answer the following questions to check your understanding of the lesson.

Use the photo of the plasma globe to answer Questions 3 and 4.

3. Once a gas's temperature rises above a certain point, its particles start to break apart and it becomes plasma. Plasma can generate and be affected by electric and magnetic fields. The plasma streams inside the globe are evidence that an electric field *acts throughout the globe. / only acts in the center of the globe.*

   When a person touches the glass globe, he or she affects the pattern of the plasma because of the electric force between their hands and the plasma inside the glass. This is evidence that the electric field acts on objects *that are touching / at a distance.*

4. A student learns that an LED bulb will light up when it is in the electric field of a plasma globe. What steps will help the student map and model the field during an experiment? Select all steps that apply.

   A. Observe how the plasma moves inside the globe.

   B. Walk around the globe, recording where the LED bulb lights up.

   C. Move the LED bulb closer to the plasma globe until it lights up.

   D. Measure the distance between the glowing LED bulb and the plasma globe.

Use the photo of the 3D magnetic field to answer Questions 5 and 6.

5. What does the photo show about the magnetic field around the magnet? Select all statements that apply.

   A. The magnet can attract iron filings without touching them.

   B. The magnetic field around the magnet is strongest at its poles.

   C. The strength of the magnetic field is the same throughout the liquid.

   D. The magnetic field is three dimensional.

6. The magnetic field is *strongest / weakest* near the poles of the magnet.

Interactive Review

Complete this section to review the main concepts of the lesson.

The area in which an object experiences a noncontact force is called a field. Examples of fields include electric fields, magnetic fields, and gravitational fields. A field extends throughout space and lessens with distance until it is undetectable. Fields are measurable and follow the motion of the field's source.

A. In your own words, explain what a field is in science. Use examples to support your explanation.

The density of field lines models the strength of a field. For example, equally spaced field lines model a uniform field. Field lines that are close together model a strong field whereas field lines that are widely spaced model a weak field.

B. Create a checklist of important points to remember when modeling a magnetic field.

Electromagnetism

An MRI machine produces a strong magnetic field, which is used to generate images of the inside of a person's body.

By the end of this lesson . . .

you will be able to analyze electromagnetic data to explain the interaction between electric and magnetic phenomena.

Go online to view the digital version of the Hands-On Lab for this lesson and to download additional lab resources.

CAN YOU EXPLAIN IT?

How can these pieces of metal be picked up and then released without the crane grabbing them from their sides or bottom?

Cranes such as the one pictured are used to move scrap metal. These cranes are able to lift heavy metal objects, move the objects to another place, and then release them. These cranes are able to pick up these objects without grabbing them from their sides or bottom.

Explore ONLINE!

1. How might the crane be picking up these pieces of metal?

2. What does the crane's ability to release the pieces of metal indicate about how it is picking up these objects?

 EVIDENCE NOTEBOOK As you explore the lesson, gather evidence to help explain how the crane can lift and release these metal objects.

Explaining Electric Current

Charge Movement

In many cases, a large number of electric charges move through objects at the same time. When many charges are moving, measuring individual charges becomes difficult and less useful.

3. **Discuss** With a partner, determine a measurement that might be more useful than measuring the movement of an individual charge.

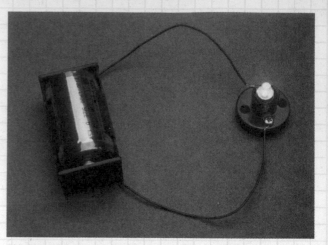

The electric charges flowing through this light bulb cause it to light up.

Current

The movement of electric charges is key to many phenomena. To describe this movement, the term *current* is used. An **electric current** is a continuous flow of electric charges from one region to another. An electric current can be measured by determining the rate at which electric charges move past a certain point.

Moving Charge

The negative electric charge in this wire moves toward a positively charged region.

Explore ONLINE!

4. **Write** In an electric current, electric charges are constantly in motion and following a path. What are some advantages of using electric current instead of individual charges to discuss the movement of charges? Relate your explanation to another situation where discussing rates of movement would be more useful than discussing the movement of individual items.

5. You cannot see an electric charge move from the hair on your head to a balloon when they are rubbed together, and you cannot see a charge moving through wire. How might we measure the movement of a charge if electric charges are not visible?

A. A physical effect of the charge's movement must be used to measure the charge.

B. Magnification must be used to see the electric charge so its movement can be measured.

C. The electric charge must be measured by the change in mass of the substance that accepts the charge.

D. The time for the electric charge to transfer must be used to measure the movement of the charge.

Ammeters

Ammeters are devices that are used to measure electric current. They measure the rate that electric charges are moving through a wire. The unit of measure of this rate is called an ampere, or amp. The amp is a measure of the amount of electric charge that passes a particular point in a given amount of time. There are several types of ammeters, but all of them use a physical effect of electric current to measure the rate of charge movement.

Ammeters allow us to visualize the effects of electric current in a wire.

Analyze Electric Heaters

When electric charge flows through an object, it can cause the object to become hotter. Many heaters operate using this phenomenon. Electric current is run through wires to warm water in electric kettles, and some portable space heaters also use electric current.

6. What might be some advantages of using an electric current to warm objects instead of other methods, such as burning wood?

_____

_____

_____

_____

_____

_____

_____

Analyzing Current and the Magnetic Force

Compasses and Electric Current

A compass is an instrument that is used to find north. The needle of a compass is a small magnet. Earth has a large (but weak in strength) magnetic field that attracts the north-seeking side of the compass needle toward the North Pole. However, when another magnet is near the needle, the needle will often be affected by that magnetic field more than Earth's magnetic field.

7. **Discuss** With a partner, discuss what conclusion you can draw from the differences between the two images of compasses.

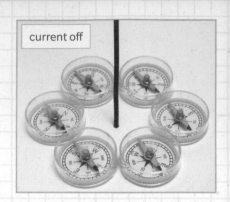

current off

current on

Moving Electric Charge and Magnetic Fields

When an electric current was passed through the wire, the compass needles moved. That is because moving electric charges generate a magnetic field. A magnetic field occurs when charged objects move or when charges move through an object. The magnetic field is only produced when the charges are moving. When the charges stop moving, the magnetic field disappears.

Moving Charge

When an electric charge moves, the charge generates a magnetic field in a loop around the moving charge.

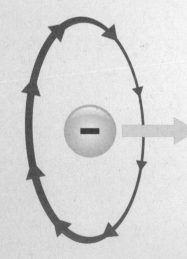

Explore ONLINE!

Electromagnetism

The interaction between electricity and magnetism is called **electromagnetism**. When electric charges move, they generate a magnetic field. Likewise, changes in the magnetic field can affect electric charges. Electric and magnetic forces are closely tied together and affect one another.

8. Electric charge and magnetism are related to one another. Magnetic fields are generated by moving / stationary electric charges. When an electric charge is stationary / in motion, there is no magnetic field. The magnetic field cannot be seen, but its effects can be observed with a light bulb / compass.

9. Recall that electric current is a movement of electric charges. If a wire is connected to an electric power source, such as a battery, electric charges will move through the wire. What will be the effect on the magnetic field around the wire as these charges move through the wire?

When no charge is moving through a wire, a magnetic field is not generated.

Electric Current and the Magnetic Field

The magnetic field that forms around a long, straight wire is in the shape of a cylinder. As many electric charges move through a wire, the magnetic fields that they each produce overlap. These overlapping fields produce a cylindrical magnetic field around the wire, along its entire length.

Recall what happened when the compasses were placed around the wire. All of the compasses pointed in a circle once there was a current in the wire. A magnetic field loop was generated around the wire while the electric charges were moving.

When charges move through the wire, a magnetic field is generated around the wire.

EVIDENCE NOTEBOOK

10. How might a magnetic force that can be turned on or off be used? Record your evidence.

Solenoids

Current in a wire produces a magnetic field. A wire producing a magnetic field does not have to be completely straight. Changing a straight wire into another shape also changes the shape of the magnetic field. One configuration is a long, straight coil of wire, called a *solenoid*. A solenoid uses loops of wire to concentrate the magnetic field into a smaller area. The loops of wire generate a stronger, smaller magnetic field than a straight wire does. A solenoid also does not have to be a series of empty loops of wire. A solenoid can be wrapped around an object, which is known as the solenoid's core.

11. Why does wrapping wire into a solenoid shape increase the strength of the magnetic field?

By looping a current-carrying wire on top of itself, the magnetic field can be concentrated in one spot.

straight wire

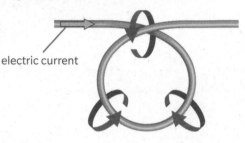

single looped wire

electric current

double looped wire

Engineer It
Explore Uses of Solenoids

12. Solenoids are often used to operate the starter switch in a car engine. When a car is turned on, electric charges flow through the solenoid. The magnetic field that the solenoid generates causes a switch to move and close. The closed switch starts the engine. What does this tell you about the material of the switch?

_____

_____

_____

_____

_____

The smaller cylinder on the top of this automobile starter motor contains a solenoid.

Measuring the Magnetic Force Due to Current

Using a solenoid instead of a straight wire is a design that increases the strength of the magnetic field generated by an electric current. Changes in the material that the coil is wrapped around can also change the strength of the magnetic field.

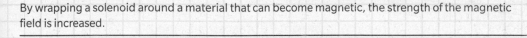

By wrapping a solenoid around a material that can become magnetic, the strength of the magnetic field is increased.

13. Why might wrapping a solenoid around an iron core produce a stronger magnetic field than wrapping a solenoid around a wooden core?

Electromagnets

An **electromagnet** is a coil of wire around an iron core. An electromagnet makes use of the magnetic field generated by an electric current in a wire, just like a solenoid. By placing a piece of iron in the middle, the force is amplified. Iron is a substance that can be made into a magnet under the right conditions. The magnetic field generated by moving charges temporarily aligns the magnetic domains of the iron, making it magnetic. The piece of iron then acts as a magnet as well. This makes an electromagnet much stronger than a solenoid without a core.

Hands-On Lab
Build an Electromagnet

You will construct an electromagnet and test its strength. You will identify possible ways in which you can improve the strength of your magnet by changing the design. Use your knowledge of electromagnetism to support your exploration.

   Electromagnets share many properties with permanent magnets. With permanent magnets, the magnetic force on an object depends on the strength of the magnet and distance between the object and magnet. The force due to an electromagnet depends on the material of the core, but there are other factors that affect the force's strength.

MATERIALS
- batteries, 1.5 volt (1-3)
- batteries, D-cell (1-3)
- nails, 4, 5, and 6 inch
- paper clips, metal
- ruler
- wire, insulated or coated, cut into assorted lengths

Procedure

STEP 1 Build an electromagnet like the one pictured on the previous page. Wrap a piece of wire around a nail 30 times to build the electromagnet. Make sure you leave enough bare wire at each end of the coil to attach the wire to a battery. Test the electromagnet's strength by measuring the distance at which the magnet will first attract a paper clip. Record the distance in the table.

STEP 2 **Engineer It** Think about some ways that you could make your electromagnet stronger. In the left column, list your design ideas to increase the strength of the electromagnet.

STEP 3 Make each design change and test it to see at what distance the magnet will attract the paper clip. Then record the distance in the table.

STEP 4 See how effective your changes were by comparing the distances measured for each design.

Electromagnet Designs	Distance
Original electromagnet	

Analysis

STEP 5 Discuss With your group, discuss your different designs. What factors seemed to affect the strength of the magnetic force generated by an electromagnet?

Electric Current and the Magnetic Force

Electric current is a factor that affects the strength of the magnetic force. Recall that current is a measurement of the rate of electric charges moving past a point. Every charge moving through the wire contributes to the magnetic field around the wire. When the current is increased, the electromagnet becomes stronger.

Explore ONLINE!

Changing Current

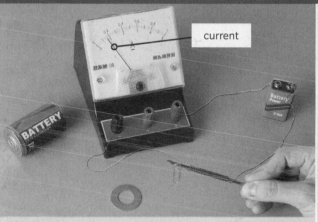

current

Running a current of 0.8 amps through this electromagnet allows it to pick up light paper clips.

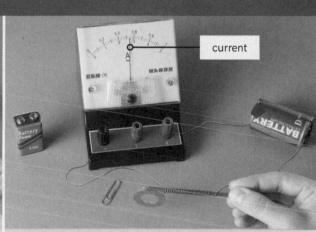

current

Running a current of 2.7 amps through the same electromagnet allows it to pick up heavier washers.

14. What conclusions can you draw about how changing the electric current in an electromagnet would affect the magnetic force generated?

EVIDENCE NOTEBOOK

15. The current in an electromagnet can be controlled. How might the ability to control the strength of an electromagnet relate to the crane's ability to pick up and release metal? Record your evidence.

Number of Loops and the Magnetic Force

The shape of the wire also affects the magnetic force. Recall that a solenoid with current running through it generates a larger magnetic force than a straight wire with a current running through it. Each portion of the wire with charge moving through it generates the same strength of magnetic field. By looping the wire, the magnetic field can be concentrated and become stronger.

Explore ONLINE!

Number of Loops

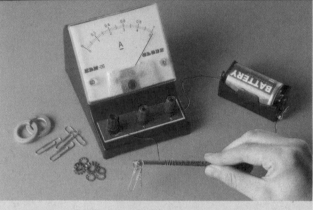 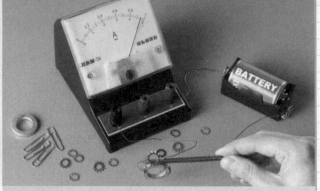

This electromagnet has 30 loops of wire wrapped around its core and can pick up light paper clips.

This electromagnet has 60 loops of wire wrapped around its core and can pick up heavier washers.

16. What conclusion can you draw about how changing the shape of the wire affects the strength of the magnetic force?

Language SmArts

Explain the Usefulness of Electromagnets

17. Electromagnets are used for many purposes, ranging from cranes to high-end brake systems for cars. What are some reasons that an electromagnet might be more useful than a permanent magnet in many situations? Support your answer with evidence from the text and your own experiences.

_____

_____

_____

_____

EVIDENCE NOTEBOOK

18. Consider how the electromagnets you've seen are used. Are any of them used in similar ways to a crane that picks up scrap metal? Record your evidence.

Measuring the Current Due to a Magnetic Field

Magnetic Field and Current

When electric charges move, they generate a magnetic field. Similarly, a moving magnet or changing magnetic field can have an effect on charges. When a magnet is moved near a wire, the effect on the charges in the wire can be observed by seeing how the current changes.

▷ *Explore ONLINE!*

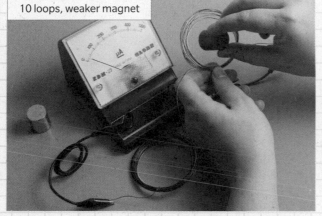

10 loops, weaker magnet

A weaker magnet is moved toward 10 loops of wire, generating a maximum current of 20 microamps in the wire.

30 loops, weaker magnet

A weaker magnet is moved toward 30 loops of wire, generating a maximum current of 40 microamps in the wire.

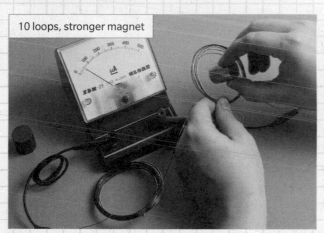

10 loops, stronger magnet

A stronger magnet is moved toward 10 loops of wire, generating a maximum current of 50 microamps in the wire.

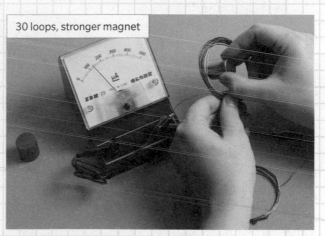

30 loops, stronger magnet

A stronger magnet is moved toward 30 loops of wire, generating a maximum current of 140 microamps in the wire.

19. Using the photos and your knowledge of electromagnetism, select the factors that might affect the amount of current displayed on the ammeter.

   A. the number of loops in the solenoid

   B. the speed of the magnet's movement

   C. the magnet used

   D. whether the magnet touches the solenoid

Electromagnetic Induction

When a magnetic field changes near electric charges, a force is generated on those charges. This force can cause electric charges to move. This is known as **electromagnetic induction**. When a current is generated by a changing magnetic field, we say the current is induced.

Change in a Magnetic Field and Current

The amount of current induced in a wire is directly related to how the magnetic field around the wire changes. When a magnet moves quickly near a wire, the magnetic field around the wire changes by a large amount. When a magnet moves slowly near a wire, the magnetic field around the wire changes slowly and less current is induced. A magnet's strength can also affect the amount of current induced in the wire. A strong magnet produces a stronger magnetic field. A small movement of a strong magnet can produce a large change in the magnetic field around the wire.

20. Using a stronger magnet will create a smaller / larger change in the magnetic field and cause the charges to move slower / faster. Moving the magnet more slowly will create a smaller / larger change in the motion of the electric charges.

Current and Magnetic Field

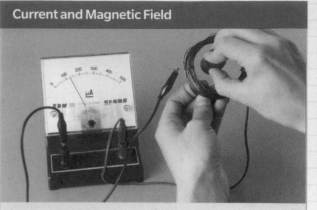

When this magnet is moved through this loop of wire, it generates a maximum current of 130 microamps.

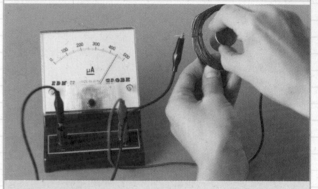

A stronger magnet moved through the same loop of wire generates a maximum current of 440 microamps.

Explore ONLINE!

Number of Loops and Current

The amount of current induced in a wire depends on the number of loops in the wire. When a current is run through a solenoid, the loops of the wire amplify the magnetic field of the wire. Here, when the wire is looped, more of the wire is affected by a change in the magnetic field. Increasing the number of loops increases the number of charges in the wire that are affected by a change in the magnetic field.

Current and Number of Loops

Moving this magnet through 10 loops of wire generates a maximum current of 40 microamps.

Moving this magnet through 20 loops of wire generates a maximum current of 90 microamps.

Moving this magnet through 30 loops of wire generates a maximum current of 140 microamps.

Do the Math

Analyze Measurements of Current

The relationship between the number of loops in a solenoid and the current that is induced in the wire by a magnet can be found by graphing the data. Use the images provided at the bottom of the previous page as your data points.

21. Fill in the table using the data from the pictures provided on the previous page.

Number of Loops	Current (microamps)

22. Make a graph that shows the relationship between the number of loops and the induced electric current. The graph should show the number of loops on the x-axis and the induced current on the y-axis. Because the photos showed three different solenoids, you should have three data points.

23. From your graph, what conclusion can you draw about how the number of loops of the solenoid affects the amount of electric current induced?

   A. More loops in the solenoid increases the electric current induced.

   B. More loops in the solenoid decreases the electric current induced.

   C. The number of loops in the solenoid does not affect the electric current induced.

Induced Current

When a magnet or loop of wire moves relative to the other, a current is induced in the loop of wire.

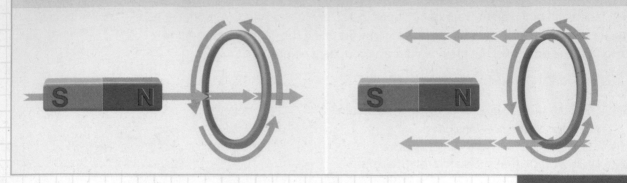

24. Do you think it matters whether the wire or the magnet is moved to induce an electric current? Explain your answer.

Explore ONLINE!

Induction and Reference Frames

A current can be induced in a wire if either the magnet or the wire is moving. The two must be moving in relation to one another. If the magnet is motionless and the wire moves, a current will be induced. If the wire is motionless and the magnet moves, a current will be induced. If both the magnet and the wire move in relation to one another, a current will be induced. However, if both the magnet and the wire have the same velocity, a current will not be induced. If the magnet and wire are moving at the same velocity, they are moving at the same speed in the same direction. The two objects would not be moving in relation to one another, and a current would not be induced.

Explore Uses of Induced Electric Current

25. What is commonly referred to as "electricity" is caused by the movement of electric charges. Induced electric current is used in electric generators and the power grid to move these charges. What might make induced current so useful for supplying electric power when compared to other methods, such as batteries?

_____

_____

_____

_____

_____

_____

_____

Continue Your Exploration

Name: _____   Date: _____

Check out the path below or go online to choose one of the other paths shown.

Careers in Science

- **Hands-On Labs** ✋
- **Generators and Energy Resources**
- **Propose Your Own Path**

Go online to choose one of these other paths.

MRI Technician

The use of electromagnetism has expanded our capabilities in many areas, including the medical field. One step forward in the medical field was the invention of magnetic resonance imaging (MRI) machines. MRI machines use powerful magnetic fields to generate images of organs. MRI technicians operate these machines and work with patients and doctors to produce accurate images for diagnoses.

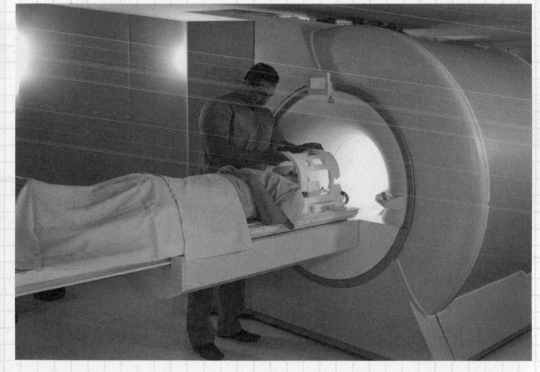

MRI technicians use MRI machines to produce images of the inside of a patient's body. In addition to operating an MRI machine, technicians also interact with patients and doctors.

1. MRI machines use extremely strong magnetic fields. These fields must be adjustable to produce high-quality images. What might these machines use to generate such a field?

   A. permanent magnets

   B. electromagnets

   C. induced current

Continue Your Exploration

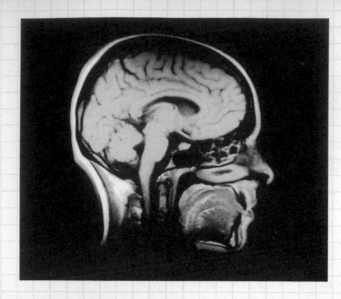

An MRI machine takes images of several cross-sections of a person's body, which can be combined to generate a three-dimensional representation.

2. Why might the ability to produce three-dimensional images of organs be helpful in diagnosing a patient's ailment?

3. MRI machines excite hydrogen atoms in a person's body and then detect them to generate images. The main source of hydrogen atoms in the human body is water. Which of the following are limitations this method might place on the images that can be generated? Choose all that apply.

   A. Detecting hydrogen atoms allows for certain types of structures to be imaged better than others.

   B. The excited hydrogen atoms in water molecules could combust.

   C. Areas without large amounts of water are harder to map.

4. When MRI machines are capturing images of a person's body, they produce extremely powerful magnetic fields. What might be some issues that an MRI technician would need to work around due to these magnetic fields?

5. **Collaborate** With a partner, discuss how the ability to generate images of the inside of a person's body may have advanced our understanding of diseases and improved our diagnosis and treatment abilities.

Can You Explain It?

Name: _____   **Date:** _____

How can these pieces of metal be picked up and then released without the crane grabbing them from their sides or bottom?

Explore ONLINE!

 EVIDENCE NOTEBOOK

Refer to the notes in your Evidence Notebook to help you construct an explanation for how the crane is able to pick up and release the scrap metal.

1. State your claim. Make sure your claim fully explains how electromagnetism is used to make a crane operate.

2. Summarize the evidence you have gathered to support your claim and explain your reasoning.

Checkpoints

Answer the following questions to check your understanding of the lesson.

Use the image to answer Question 3.

3. The electromagnet and permanent magnet pictured are equal in strength. How could the force between the two magnets be increased? Choose all that apply.

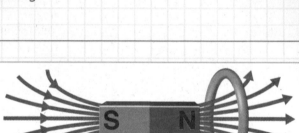

   A. The magnets could be moved closer together.

   B. The current in the electromagnet could be decreased.

   C. The permanent magnet could be turned around.

   D. The number of loops in the electromagnet could be increased.

4. Which statement describes the current on the surface of a balloon that is charged with static electricity?

   A. There is no current because the charges are only on the surface of the balloon.

   B. The current is high because the charges are separated.

   C. There is no current because the charges are not moving.

Use the image to answer Questions 5 and 6.

5. The permanent magnet is being moved toward the wire. If the permanent magnet is accelerated as it moves toward the wire, what will happen to the induced current in the wire?

   A. The current decreases as the magnet moves faster.

   B. The current increases as the magnet moves faster.

   C. There is no current in the wire.

6. If the permanent magnet were to be doubled in size and then placed so that it was touching the loop of wire, what statement could be said about the current in the loop of wire?

   A. The current would double in magnitude due to the larger magnet.

   B. The current would increase due to the magnet contacting the wire.

   C. There would be no current in the wire due to the stationary magnet.

Interactive Review

Complete this study guide to review the lesson.

Current is the measure of the rate of charges moving past a specific point. Current can be measured using an ammeter.

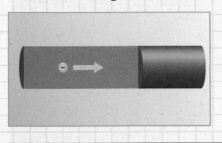

A. An ammeter is used to measure the current in a wire. If an ammeter indicates a current in a wire, what can be said about the charges in the wire?

Electromagnetism is the interaction between electric and magnetic phenomena. Moving electric charges create a magnetic force.

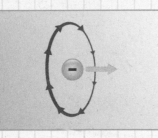

B. Making loops in a wire with a current running through it increases the strength of the magnetic field around the loop. What happens to the magnetic field generated by other straight parts of the wire?

An electromagnet is a coil of wire wrapped around an iron core. An electromagnet's strength is affected by the shape of the wire and the current in the wire.

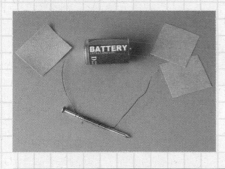

C. How does an increase in the amount of charge flowing through an electromagnet change the current and the magnetic force generated by the current?

Changing magnetic fields causes electric charges to move. These moving charges can be measured as a change in current.

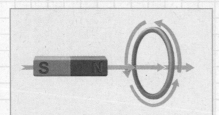

D. Explain how you could increase the amount of current induced in a wire.

Choose one of the activities to explore how this unit connects to other topics.

☐ Earth Science Connection

Earth's Fireworks Have you ever seen a photograph like this? Perhaps you have seen this phenomenon in person. Auroras, also called northern or southern lights, are beautiful displays of light in the sky caused by electric and magnetic forces in Earth's atmosphere.

Research how electric and magnetic forces create auroras, and prepare a digital presentation explaining how scientists can predict when and where they will occur. Include images in your presentation.

☐ Social Studies Connection

History of Electromagnetism Today we have countless uses for electromagnets, ranging from large industrial machinery to small electronic components. Scientists have worked to better understand electromagnets and develop practical uses for them. When did people first discover the relationship between electric and magnetic forces?

Research how electromagnets were invented and how they have been developed over the past two hundred years. Present your information in the form of a timeline chart, with one column listing dates and the other column key developments in understanding electromagnetism. Include examples of uses for electromagnets.

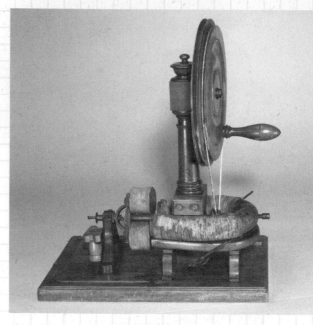

☐ Technology Connection

Electromagnets in Technology We love our modern technology. However, without an understanding of electric and magnetic forces, we would not have these amazing devices. Electromagnets are used in technology ranging from transportation to medicine to scientific research.

Research one example of modern technology that uses electromagnets. Explain how electromagnets make the technology work and the criteria and constraints involved in its design. Present your findings to the class.

Name: _____   Date: _____

Use Diagrams A and B to answer Questions 1–3.

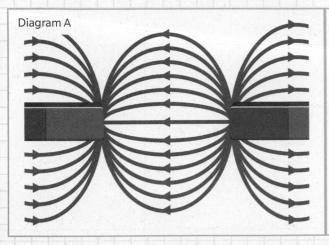

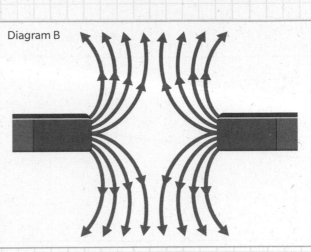

1. Which of the following is the best explanation for Diagram A?

   A. The field lines connect the objects due to a repulsive force.

   B. The field lines diverge due to a repulsive force.

   C. The field lines connect the objects due to an attractive force.

   D. The field lines diverge due to an attractive force.

2. Which of the following is the best explanation for Diagram B?

   A. The field lines connect the objects due to a repulsive force.

   B. The field lines diverge due to a repulsive force.

   C. The field lines connect the objects due to an attractive force.

   D. The field lines diverge due to an attractive force.

3. Which of the following sets of objects would produce field lines similar to those in Diagram A? Select all that apply.

   A. Two magnets with the N poles facing each other

   B. Two magnets with the N and S poles facing each other

   C. Two oppositely charged objects

   D. Two objects with positive charges

4. Moving two magnetic objects closer together will *not change / increase / decrease* the strength of the magnetic force between them.

5. Two balloons charged with static electricity move away from each other when placed side-by-side. Which statement best explains this phenomenon?

   A. The balloons have opposite electric charges, creating an attractive electric force.

   B. The balloons have like electric charges, creating an attractive electric force.

   C. The balloons have opposite electric charges, creating a repulsive electric force.

   D. The balloons have like electric charges, creating a repulsive electric force.

6. Complete the table by providing descriptions of how each of these phenomena relate to each big picture concept.

Phenomenon	Predictable Patterns of Behavior	Cause and Effect	Real-World Applications
Electric currents			
Magnetic attraction and repulsion			
Static electricity			
Electromagnetic forces			

Name: _____   Date: _____

Use the images to answer Questions 7–10.

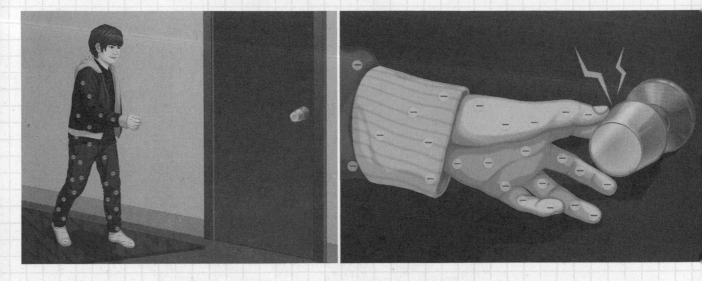

7. The image depicts an example of static electricity. Explain the meaning of static electricity.

8. Touching the doorknob sent a shock to the person's hand. What is this called, and what is happening with the charges?

9. Why does a person's hand have to be close to the doorknob in order for the electric discharge (shock) to occur? Why doesn't this occur from across the room?

10. How is this example of static electricity related to lightning during a thunderstorm?

Use the diagram to answer Questions 11–14.

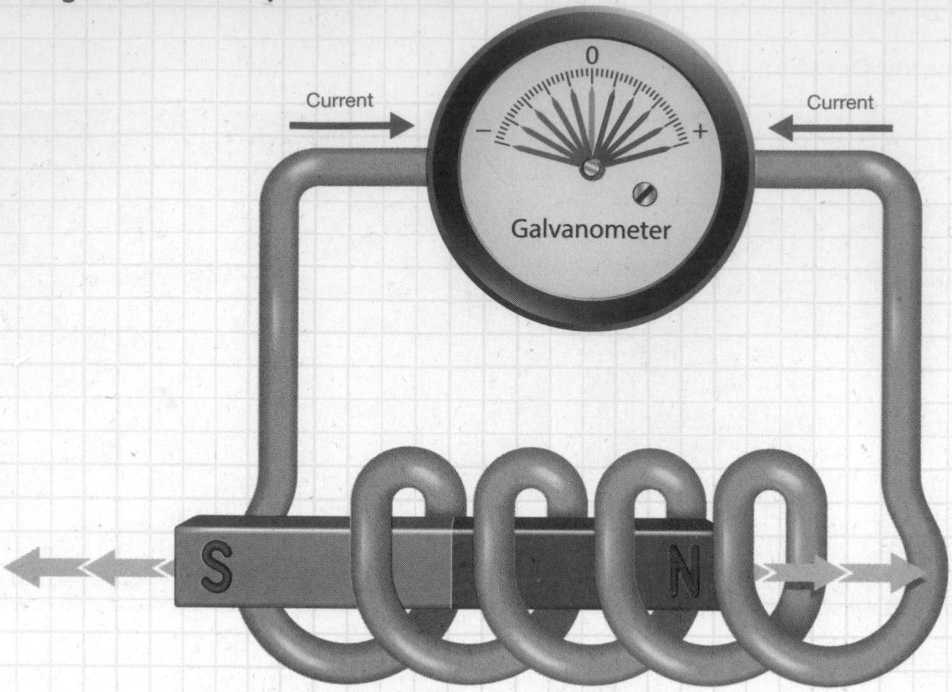

Current

Current

0

Galvanometer

S   N

11. What is the effect of moving the magnet back and forth inside the coiled wire?

12. Would moving the coil back and forth instead of the magnet produce the same effect? Explain.

13. Predict what would happen if the entire unit is moving, but the magnet and coil are not moving relative to each other.

14. Describe ways to increase the amount of electric current in this setup.

Name: _____   Date: _____

What is the best design for a maglev train?

Have you ever seen a floating train? Trains that use magnetic levitation (maglev) are suspended above the track, which greatly reduces friction from the rails and allows the trains to travel between 250 and 300 miles per hour! Magnetic levitation uses attractive and repulsive magnetic forces to suspend and control the speeds and motion of the trains.

Using your knowledge of electromagnets, design a maglev train that can move forward and backward. Follow the steps below to help you through the engineering design process.

The steps below will help guide your research and develop your recommendation.

Engineer It

1. **Define the Problem** Write a statement defining the problem you have been asked to solve. What are the criteria and constraints involved in designing a maglev train?

Engineer It

2. **Conduct Research** To get ideas for your design, research existing maglev trains. Find out how magnets are positioned in order to achieve both levitation and back-and-forth motion. Describe how electric and magnetic forces are used in these systems.

3. **Analyze and Evaluate Research** Use ideas from the models you researched and your knowledge of electric and magnetic forces to create your own design. Your analysis of the research should help you decide where and how the magnets should be positioned to achieve both levitation and back-and-forth motion.

4. **Create a Model** On a separate sheet of paper, draw a diagram that shows all of the components for your maglev train. Be sure to label the components, including a legend or key if needed. Make certain to indicate how the train can move forward and backward.

5. **Communicate** On a separate sheet of paper, write a brief report to accompany your diagram. In the report, describe how your maglev train works and your reasons for choosing this particular design.

✓ Self-Check

	I identified the problem.
	I researched existing maglev systems to get ideas for my design.
	I designed a model using ideas from existing systems and my knowledge of electric and magnetic forces.
	My design was clearly communicated to others.

Glossary

Pronunciation Key							
Sound	**Symbol**	**Example**	**Respelling**	**Sound**	**Symbol**	**Example**	**Respelling**
ă	a	pat	PAT	ŏ	ah	bottle	BAHT'l
ā	ay	pay	PAY	ō	oh	toe	TOH
âr	air	care	KAIR	ô	aw	caught	KAWT
ä	ah	father	FAH•ther	ôr	ohr	roar	ROHR
är	ar	argue	AR•gyoo	oi	oy	noisy	NOYZ•ee
ch	ch	chase	CHAYS	ŏŏ	u	book	BUK
ĕ	e	pet	PET	ōō	oo	boot	BOOT
ĕ (at end of a syllable)	eh	settee lessee	seh•TEE leh•SEE	ou	ow	pound	POWND
ĕr	ehr	merry	MEHR•ee	s	s	center	SEN•ter
ē	ee	beach	BEECH	sh	sh	cache	CASH
g	g	gas	GAS	ŭ	uh	flood	FLUHD
ĭ	i	pit	PIT	ûr	er	bird	BERD
ĭ (at end of a syllable)	ih	guitar	gih•TAR	z	z	xylophone	ZY•luh•fohn
ī	y eye (only for a complete syllable)	pie island	PY EYE•luhnd	z	z	bags	BAGZ
îr	ir	hear	HIR	zh	zh	decision	dih•SIZH•uhn
j	j	germ	JERM	ə	uh	around broken focus	uh•ROWND BROH•kuhn FOH•kuhs
k	k	kick	KIK	ər	er	winner	WIN•er
ng	ng	thing	THING	th	th	thin they	THIN THAY
ngk	ngk	bank	BANGK	w	w	one	WUHN
				wh	hw	whether	HWETH•er

acceleration (ak•sel•uh•RAY•shuhn)

the rate at which velocity changes over time; an object accelerates if its speed, direction, or both change (9, 50)

aceleración la tasa a la que la velocidad cambia con el tiempo; un objeto acelera si su rapidez cambia, si su dirección cambia, o si tanto su rapidez como su dirección cambian

electric charge (ee•LEK•trik CHARJ)

a fundamental property of matter that leads to the electromagnetic interactions between particles that make up matter (114)

carga eléctrica propiedad fundamental de la materia que genera las interacciones electromagnéticas entre las partículas que componen la materia

electric current (ee•LEK•trik KER•uhnt)

the rate at which electric charges pass a given point (150)

corriente eléctrica la tasa a la que las cargas eléctricas pasan por un punto dado

electric field (ee•LEK•trik FEELD)

the space around a charged object in which another charged object experiences an electric force (135)

campo eléctrico el espacio que se encuentra alrededor de un objeto con carga y en el que otro objeto con carga experimenta una fuerza eléctrica

electric force (ee•LEK•trik FOHRS)

the force of attraction or repulsion on a charged particle (118)

fuerza eléctrica fuerza de atracción o repulsión sobre una partícula cargada

electromagnet (ee•lek•troh•MAG•nit)

a coil that has a soft iron core and that acts as a magnet when an electric current is in the coil (155)

electroimán una bobina que tiene un centro de hierro suave y que funciona como un imán cuando hay una corriente eléctrica en la bobina

electromagnetic induction (ee•lek•troh•mag•NET•ik in•DUHK•shuhn)

the process of creating a current in a circuit by changing a magnetic field (160)

inducción electromagnética el proceso de crear una corriente en un circuito por medio de un cambio en el campo magnético

electromagnetism (ee•lek•troh•MAG•nih•tiz•uhm)

the interaction between electricity and magnetism (153)

electromagnetismo la interacción entre la electricidad y el magnetismo

field (FEELD)

any region in which a physical force has an effect (132)

campo de fuerza cualquier región en la que se efectúa una fuerza física

force (FOHRS)

a push or a pull exerted on an object that may change the motion or shape of the object; force has strength and direction (6)

fuerza un empuje o tirón que se ejerce sobre un objeto y que puede cambiar el movimiento o la forma del objeto; la fuerza tiene magnitud y dirección

friction (FRIK•shuhn)

a force that opposes motion between two surfaces that are in contact (32)

fricción una fuerza que se opone al movimiento entre dos superficies que están en contacto

gravitational field (grav•ih•TAY•shuh•nuhl FEELD)

the area surrounding a mass in which another mass would be influenced by a force of gravitational attraction (134)

campo gravitacional área que rodea una masa en la cual otra masa se vería influenciada por una fuerza de atracción gravitacional

gravity (GRAV•ih•tee)

a force of attraction between objects that is due to their masses and that decreases as the distance between the objects increases (26)

gravedad una fuerza de atracción entre dos objetos debida a sus masas, que disminuye a medida que la distancia entre los objetos aumenta

inertia (ih•NER•shuh)

the tendency of an object to resist changes in motion (53)

inercia la tendencia de un objeto a resistir cambios en su movimiento sobre el objeto

magnet (MAG•nit)

any material that attracts iron or materials containing iron (98)

imán cualquier material que atrae hierro o materiales que contienen hierro

magnetic domain (mag•NET•ik doh•MAYN)

a region composed of a group of atoms whose magnetic fields are aligned in the same direction (105)

dominio magnético una región compuesta por un grupo de átomos cuyos campos magnéticos están alineados en la misma dirección

magnetic field (mag•NET•ik FEELD)

a region where a magnetic force can be detected (137)

campo magnético una región donde puede detectarse una fuerza magnética

magnetic force (mag•NET•ik FOHRS)

the force of attraction or repulsion generated by magnetic material (98)

fuerza magnética fuerza de atracción o repulsión generada por material magnético

motion (MOH•shuhn)
   an object's change in position relative to a
   reference point (46)
   movimiento el cambio en la posición de un objeto
   respecto a un punto de referencia

newton (NOOT•n)
   the SI unit for force (symbol, N) (7)
   newton la unidad de fuerza del sistema internacional de
   unidades (símbolo: N)

reference point (REF•er•uhns POYNT)
   a location to which another location is compared (47)
   punto de referencia una ubicación con la que se compara
   otra ubicación

speed (SPEED)
   the distance traveled divided by the time interval during
   which the motion occurred (47)
   rapidez la distancia que un objeto se desplaza dividida
   entre el intervalo de tiempo durante el cual ocurrió el
   movimiento

velocity (vuh•LAHS•ih•tee)
   the speed of an object in a particular direction (9)
   velocidad la rapidez de un objeto en una dirección dada

Index

Note: Italic page numbers represent illustrative material, such as figures, tables, margin elements, photographs, and illustrations. Boldface page numbers represent page numbers for definitions.